HOW TO
SELECT A
BUSINESS SITE

HOW TO SELECT A BUSINESS SITE

The Executive's Location Guide

Jon E. Browning

(with cooperation of The Rouse Company)

McGraw-Hill Company

New York St. Louis San Francisco Auckland
Bogotá Hamburg Johannesburg London
Madrid Mexico Montreal New Dehli
Panama São Paulo Singapore
Sydney Tokyo Paris
Toronto

Library of Congress Cataloging in Publication Data

Browning, Jon E.
  How to select a business site.

  Bibliography: p.
  Includes index.
  1. Business relocation. 2. Industries, Location
of. I. Title.
HD58.B76   658.2'1   79-19414
ISBN 0-07-008495-5

The editors for this book were Robert L. Davidson and Susan
Thomas, the designer was Mark E. Safran, and the production
supervisor was Sally Fliess. It was set in Electra by University
Graphics, Inc.

Printed and bound by The Book Press.

Contents

Contents

Foreword

One of the most momentous decisions any manager will ever make—whether running a multibillion dollar conglomerate or a neighborhood clothing store—is the decision to move the business or any part of it.

Whether it means shifting a plant, an office, a warehouse or a showroom, anyone who faces such a decision must live with the consequences for a long, long time. Most firms that move at all move only once or twice in a business lifetime. So if you have ever executed such a move (and it would not be at all unusual if you hadn't), you probably did it many years ago. Whatever a manager's past experience in planning company moves, there is clearly a need for good, sound, up-to-the-minute counsel.

Hence this book. Its objective is simple: to guide you through one of the most complex and important decisions you will ever be called upon to make and carry out. Of course, a book like *How to Select a Business Site* is only a first step in preparing for effective decision making on a business move. By consulting with real estate professionals who specialize in business and industrial properties, the executive will still more easily find a way through the complex maze of moving or expanding.

Moving a business, obviously, is more than just packing up the files and the typewriters, calling a truck, and setting up shop someplace new. The multitude of factors that go into a decision to move demands that the executive consider at least these questions:

- Do I really need to move—or can my space needs be met by expansion or by a new building on my present site?
- What are my actual needs? And, for comparison, what can I *afford* to do?
- Where shall I look for a new site?
- What is it going to cost me to do business at my prospective new location? What's the tax picture? And what about utilities?
- What's the attitude of the local government toward industrial development?
- How am I going to manage the transfer of my employees?
- Is the kind and quantity of labor I need available in my new location?
- What's the "quality of life" there—will my employees *want* to live and work in the new location?
- How am I going to finance my move or my purchase?

Only when all of these, and many more, questions are adequately answered does the mechanical problem of actually moving come to the fore.

The executive looking for all-purpose rules and answers won't find them in this book, for the simple reason that there are no hard-and-fast rules, no easy, universally applicable answers.

Instead, *How to Select a Business Site* offers advice based on actual experience. It shows how the managers of successful moves have solved their problems and developed the strategies and resources they needed. We believe, however, that their experiences contain at least some elements of universality—ways of approaching and making a move that can be of value to other business executives.

Actually, when you try to select a new location for your headquarters, for example, you are really seeking to determine what you want the face of your company to look like ten, twenty, or thirty years in the future.

When you view the decision-making process this way, the primacy of the so-called "subjective" factors in a real estate decision becomes clearer—factors like the quality of schools, parks, police and fire protection, recreational facilities, and other resources available in a new community. Such factors, difficult to measure, aren't supposed to affect the bottom line, but every manager knows they do. That's why they are not given short shrift in this guide.

Moving a business means moving *people*, and this book pays full attention to the problems that come along with moving individual human beings into new settings. As the decision maker, you really face a twofold task: first, to make the move as though you were moving a business, with a cold, hard eye for dollars and cents, resources, and opportunities; second, to make the move as though you were moving your family, looking at the way life will be lived in the new location. The truth is, you are actually making these two kinds of moves simultaneously.

Every year, thousands of such decisions are made. They

affect the profits and sometimes the very existence of companies large and small. Most turn out happily. The move somehow is survived and business continues in the new location successfully, productively, and profitably. Some, inevitably, go wrong, and many executives are hurt, and hurt badly, each year by faulty real estate decisions—or by faulty execution of sound decisions.

There is simply no substitute for sound, informed, and concerned advice. You can get it from professional industrial realtors whose business it is to be expert in these matters. And you can get it from those executives who have managed a successful move. That's what this book is all about.

It's not just a matter of providing the solace of numbers for executives on the move—to assure them that others have faced the same problems they now face and have found solutions, or have made their mistakes along the way. If this book has one goal it is to be *useful*. By bringing together in a single volume the combined and varied experiences of many managers who have moved their businesses successfully—along with a few who have stumbled—this book makes available a fund of information and ideas to be drawn upon as guides to decision making and action.

By studying these experiences, you will be better able to plan and implement a move that will leave you and your company in a strong position, comfortably settled, and ready to get back to the serious business of business.

Hugh J. Zimmer
President 1978–1979
Society of Industrial Realtors

Preface

Despite the importance of corporate moves and expansions and their frequency, more than two decades have gone by since a definitive guide has been published discussing how to go about finding and evaluating a location. In that time, many changes (e.g., energy) have come to affect the criteria for making a choice. This book attempts to identify the areas of concern and strategic thinking that should go into the relocation or expansion decision-making process, including the final site selection.

Although each experience is unique, there are many common elements, and these form the basis for this book. Our research tapped the numerous magazine and newspaper articles and dissertations that have looked at special segments of the problems or recounted a case history of a corporate move. In addition to drawing upon our own experience, we gleaned information from interviews with executives of the more than 900 businesses that recently chose to locate in the new city of Columbia, which is situated in Howard County, Maryland, a county known for its forward thinking and probusiness programs.

Maryland's economic development programs serve as examples of the type of assistance states can provide in the search for a suitable location and in financing the facility. On the southern fringe of the Middle Atlantic group of states and the northern end of the Southern states, Maryland has programs similar to those of other areas pursuing new payrolls and investments.

Acknowledgments

This book on relocation could not have been written without the help of many people. I owe a special debt to the staff of The Rouse Company, who shared their extensive experiences in the relocation of more than 900 companies to the new city of Columbia, Maryland and who arranged interviews with some of the executives of those firms and with state executives.

A special thanks also goes to James W. Rouse, Chairman of the Board of The Rouse Company, who shared his special insights into the social and economic factors that shape the personality of a business community. Columbia has pioneered and perfected a number of industrial and residential development concepts that serve as a model for today's city planners. Deserving of special mention is James O. Roberson, formerly in charge of new business development for the Columbia project and presently Secretary of Maryland's Department of Economic & Community Development.

All of us who have been involved personally in a move owe particular thanks to our spouses who shed their tears in private, making the move easy and the new house a home. My wife, Alice, provides the continuing love and support that makes wherever we live a continual joy and the writing of a book such as this possible.

ONE

Getting Organized

Few business decisions will have as significant and long-term an impact on a company as the decision to relocate or expand. A corporation's profits, and its people, will probably feel the impact for at least twenty years.

What a company wants from a given location will depend, of course, on the type and size of installation planned.

Over the years, markets and labor have ranked as the "most important" factors in a relocation or expansion decision for manufacturers. Recently, the availability of energy and fuel has vied for equal atttention. And the transportation network and access to raw materials round out the top five decision factors.

For a headquarters, service, or R&D facility, people are the chief resource. Thus, heading the "most wanted" list usually will be the availability of executive and professional talent. Also of high interest: the availability of good highway, air, and/or rail transportation that will make it easy for employees and customers to reach the facility.

With any relocation or expansion, regardless of how or why the site is selected, people eventually have to be uprooted from one place and transferred to another. At the same time, the company has to move its records and equipment from the old location to the new. Methods for accomplishing these transfers while avoiding common mistakes will be suggested.

KICKING OFF THE SEARCH

The corporate executive responsible for the relocation plan should start by assembling a small team of experts who can examine the labor makeup, the tax structure, and the distribution characteristics of alternative areas. The team should be fully cognizant of why the company has decided to relocate and expand and what factors will go into the final decision. If it's a headquarters move and the chief executive wants to live where sailing is handy, admit it; otherwise, a lot of work hours may be wasted weighing the pros and cons of locations miles from a suitable body of water.

Throughout the analysis process the team members should be encouraged to challenge the original assumptions by management. The company may be planning to build a new manufacturing plant when what's really needed is a new warehouse. It may be that, to take advantage of the economics of scale, existing plants should be closed down and a single large plant constructed rather than another regional plant. Or perhaps existing multiproduct plants could be converted into single-product plants and the same economics of scale achieved without the investment in new plant and the attendant costs this can entail.

In a sum, the relocation or expansion problem forces a

company to ask itself if its current way of doing business is the best way. One of the first steps may well be the reengineering of the process or a redesign of the work flow.

Figure 1 provides an ordered look at the steps involved in moving a nonmanufacturing operation. The initial analysis takes place at two levels: (1) looking at the kind and cost of existing corporate real estate and (2) analyzing the current use of space. Once the status quo has been determined, the exploration of future needs and possible real estate alternatives can proceed. Then the best options and their costs can be presented to management.

If there is a common pitfall among location decision makers, it may well be that few look closely at the kind of community in which they plan to put a new facility. Concentrating just on marketing figures or the availability of certain skilled workers may prove to be very shortsighted when considering the long-term impact of the location decision.

In a study recently completed for *The Wall Street Journal*, readers involved in making facility relocation decisions were asked to identify the type of information they seek from area development advertising.[1] Less than 10 percent of the respondents indicated that they sought information dealing with growth trends, population, financing, economic data, community attitudes, climate, living conditions, housing, and education capabilities.

But times *have* changed, although the thinking of some location decision makers has not. As American workers have become increasingly mobile, they have learned that they can usually work where they want to live—the reverse of several years ago when they had to live where they could find work. Complicating the moving decision of the individual married male worker is the fact that half of American

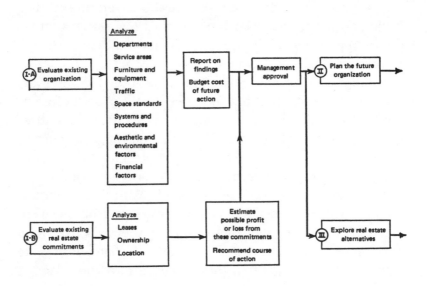

FIG. 1 Project control chart for relocation planners. (SOURCE: Michael Saphier, *Planning the New Office*, McGraw-Hill, New York, 1978, pp. 50–51.)

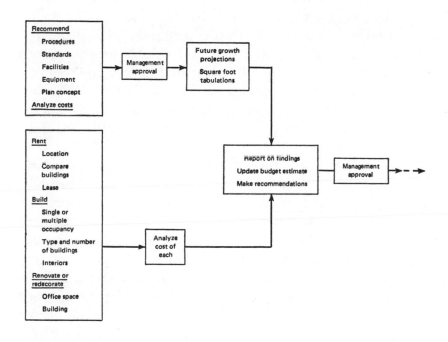

women of working age now hold a job or seek one—a job the woman may not be readily willing to give up just because a corporation decides it wants to transfer her husband.

For the dynamic, growth-oriented company (probably the company seeking additional facilities), it is critical not only to attract the very best people but also to retain them. As a result, the very rural location that offers shelter from high hourly wages, aggressive unions, or expensive taxation may also offer little attraction to the highly skilled and highly motivated employees who can find suitable jobs in more stimulating surroundings. To put it another way, the bucolic splendor of a site that was just recently a cornfield will probably lose some of its appeal when the company discovers that key middle management people cannot be attracted and retained at essentially any price.

The ready access to good housing at affordable prices in locations with good schools, good recreational facilities, and accessible cultural activities may mean more to companies in the long run than initial savings of 10 percent on wages or 50 percent on taxes. It is easy to forget that someone has to pay for governmental services. If business doesn't pay its legitimate share, employees will have to make up the difference, or the roadways, sewage system, and other services of a community will fall into disrepair. Eventually the company pays, either in the form of higher wages or high employee turnover.

SOME WHYS AND HOWS

When considering a new facility or location, the first question is: Why? Is a move needed for more space? For a better location to improve efficiency or appearance or image? To be closer to needed services or major customers? To provide room for future growth? To consolidate scattered operations? To escape from a deteriorating or high-crime area?[2]

The next question is: How? Should the present office staff be expanded or shrunk? Should there be any changes in work flow? Can procedures be streamlined? Can any equipment improvements (e.g., in communications) be made? Can the office layout be made more efficient or more commodious? Would the same major goals be accomplished by redecorating the present quarters? If not, should you lease or build? What about buying an old building and renovating? How much space do you need to accommodate future needs? And if considerable future expansion appears possible, do you need a large facility where initially you will be both landlord and occupant?

After the whys and hows have been satisfactorily answered, the question of where can be intelligently addressed. As shown in Figure 1, exploration of the real estate alternatives can proceed while management considers organizational changes. Figure 1 provides a useful time log of where you should be and what you should be doing at various stages of the site selection process.

NOTES

1. *Business on the Move*, Dow Jones & Co., Inc., Market Research Department, 1977.
2. Michael Saphier, *Planning the New Office*, McGraw-Hill, New York, 1978.

TWO

Is This Move
Really Necessary?

What motivates a corporation to pack up its files, disrupt the lives of its employees and their families, and set up shop elsewhere?

To a large extent, the answer depends upon what part of the company will be moved. Quantitative factors such as the cost of labor, energy, and transporation and the nearness to markets and raw materials form the basis for deciding whether to relocate or expand an existing plant. Cost comparisons also enter into decisions involving where to place distribution centers, research and development laboratories, and "paper factories," such as regional or divisional offices.

"Economic considerations are not decisive, however, when it comes to moving a company headquarters,"[1] observes Herbert E. Meyer. "The costs of operating the headquarters office of a large multinational corporation do not vary much with location. For one thing, the salary scales of executives, who compose 50 percent of the average headquarters staff, depend on the industry and on the company's size as measured by sales; geography is not a factor."

There have been three distinct waves of corporate migration in the U.S. over the years. The first, which occurred in the late 1800s and carried well into this century, saw companies such as Exxon, Brunswick, and others move from their home towns to financial and communication centers such as New York City and Chicago. The second began in the early 1960s and involves the movement of well-established companies from the big city to its suburbs. For example, IBM went from New York City to Armonk, New York; and Brunswick transferred from downtown Chicago to Skokie, Illinois.

"Now," points out Meyer, "a third wave of corporate migration has begun to transplant U.S. corporations from the northern and eastern regions of the country to the South and West—roughly what has lately been labeled 'the Sunbelt.' Johns-Manville, Atlantic-Richfield, Gardner-Denver, and Greyhound are just a few of the companies that have already taken part in this newest migration. It's likely that a lot more companies will joint them before the wave crests."

As the exodus gathers momentum, it spells further trouble for the traditional headquarters cities of the Northeast and Midwest. To a great extent these cities are victims of forces they cannot control.

During the first six years of the 1970s, seventy three (almost 15 percent) of the Fortune-500 companies moved their headquarters. The most frequent reason stated was the decline of the cities. High crime rates, dirty streets, and the fact that increasing numbers of young executives offered a job at headquarters refused it have also contributed. Frequently the last straw will be the shortage of office space or scattering of offices.

An added factor, points out Meyer, "is that the development of transportation and communication technology has cut the cords that bound big corporations to the traditional headquarters cities. Top executives can work far from New York or Chicago or any huge city and still be able to roam the globe and to enjoy the services of support organizations, such as big banks and law firms, that once were readily available only to city-based operations."

Similar conclusions were made by the editors of *Site Selection Handbook* based on a survey they conducted on relocations during the period 1972–1976 of companies listed in the *Dun & Bradstreet Million Dollar Directory 1976*. Out of a total of ninety-five verified headquarters relocations, forty-one were due to interregional moves (e.g., from one section of the Northeast to another). "A number of these moves were evidently inspired by the general urban to rural trend that has been ongoing in this country for some years," they observe. "Approximately 25 of the 41 interregional relocations can be attributed to this anti-city bias. . . . The next largest number of corporate relocations were traceable to moves from the Northeast to the South and Southwest—20 in all."[2]

Another observable trend is the maintenance of an old urban address with essentially a skeleton staff while large sections of the headquarters operations are moved to the suburbs.

Apart from the special case of headquarters relocations, most locational decisions do have a clearly economic justification. And whether they are "product" or "people" factories, each move can be made better with careful planning, from the earliest consideration of the possibility until sometime after the actual transfer takes place. Even a crosstown move can be highly disruptive when not properly executed.

11

FORMAL AND INFORMAL JUDGMENTS

Businesses expand their productive capacity by adding new facilities. A fundamental rule of economics is that as long as you can invest borrowed money in an asset which yields a return greater than the interest you pay, you should borrow the money and invest it. Thus, the first decision that has to be made when considering a new facility or location is the eventual impact on the bottom line. The question of how much the new plant will add to sales is just as pertinent for service industries (such as banks) to ask as it is for goods-producing organizations. Therefore, facility location should play an important part in operations planning.

Obviously, the more money is involved, the more detailed and analytical the analysis should be.

TABLE 1   Important Formal and Informal Location Judgments

	Quantitative factors	Qualitative factors
Resources	Land costs Raw material costs Subcontracting costs Transportation costs Utility rates Labor costs Energy-fuel availability	Land availability Availability of skilled and unskilled labor Labor productivity Transportation availability
Local Conditions	Construction costs Taxes	Culture Community receptivity Worker attitudes and work ethics Unionization in area Proximity to markets Quality of life: climate, housing, recreation, schools

SOURCE: Adapted from Ronald J. Ebert and Everett E. Adam, Jr., *Business Horizons*, November 1977, p. 35.

Generally speaking, the decision factors can be grouped into two categories, as shown in Table 1: those that lend themselves to quantitative evaluation and those that tend to be judged informally by management.

The problem with today's modeling techniques, suggest Roland J. Ebert and Everett E. Adam, Jr. (members of the management faculty of the University of Missouri at Columbia), is that most tend to focus on transportation costs. "Transportation costs may or may not be the critical factor in location, depending upon resource requirements, the technological process, the product, and markets. . . . Rarely can a facility location problem of moderate complexity be solved with formal analysis only," observe Ebert and Adam. Expanding on that idea, they point out that

> The decision to locate a new facility usually means that employees will be hired from within the new locale. It also means that the organization must establish appropriate community relations to "fit into" the locale as a good neighbor and citizen. . . . The managerial style and organizational structure must be adapted to the economic, political, religious, and social differences at different locations. The facility must be aware of, and adapt to, the norms and customs of local subcultures. Whereas an authoritarian leadership and managerial style may be well suited to one location, a democratic-participative approach may be appropriate in another.[3]

Thus one very subjective decision that an executive must make is whether the company is compatible with the community. Further, each community must be examined in light of its mix of skills and the company's needs. Do you require top-level skills, middle-level skills, or low-level skills? Will a training program be needed to develop the necessary

13

skills? If the community lacks the proper mix of potential employees, a firm might want to choose another location.

In his 1956 classic book, *Plant Relocation*, Leonard C. Yaseen, chairman of Fantus Company, Inc., a New York consulting firm specializing in corporate relocations, noted that the first and perhaps most important step for the executive considering plant location is to determine honestly what makes his company "tick." Yaseen recommends preparing a company history by five-year spans, showing the chronological growth of the company, increase in number of employees, additions to floor space, and new products added. This will help the executive visualize the possible future labor needs, plant size and orientation on the site, and other factors.

Most companies consider relocation or expansion because of obsolescence or overcrowding of present facilities, shifts in markets, the inability to service customers properly or to compete profitably for business, and unduly high overhead and production costs. "Careful analysis of all cost and competitive factors in present operations," emphasizes Yaseen, "will pinpoint the test which a new location must meet."[4]

NOTES

1. Herbert E. Meyer, "Why Corporations Are on the Move," *Fortune*, May 1976, pp. 251–266, 270.

2. "Are There Discernible Trends in Corporate Headquarters Relocations?," reproduced from *Site Selection Handbook*, May 1977, pp. 93–96. No further reproduction is permitted.

3. Ronald J. Ebert and Everett E. Adam, Jr., "The Human Factor in Facilities Location Planning," *Business Horizons*, pp. 35–42.

4. Leonard C. Yaseen, *Plant Location*, American Research Council, New York, 1956, pp. 5, 9.

THREE

Assembling a
Relocation Team

Is your planned facility labor-, market-, or raw-materials oriented? For the most part, raw-materials-oriented companies
have to locate close to the source. Labor-oriented firms
requiring a special skill also have somewhat limited options
because they must usually choose a site where the skills they
need are already in use. For market-oriented companies, the
orientation can be either toward the consumer or toward
distribution.

Whatever the primary focus, the relocation team must be
capable of dealing with all of the factors that go into such a
decision-making process. Since labor ranks as the most
expensive single component in the cost of most manufacturing or service activities, a skilled personnel expert must be
one member of the team.

THE PERSONNEL-LABOR EXPERT

The personnel expert should be one who has a broad understanding of the field and the problems that can arise. At
some point, he or she should communicate with colleagues

in existing companies in the targeted areas to determine the general availability and quality of labor, the prevailing wage rates, and the militancy (or lack of it) of labor unions. A fringe benefit package that will be acceptable to the community will need to be devised. And the caliber and quality of training programs in the area will have to be evaluated, including whether any federal or state funds would be available for training prospective employees.

Perhaps the most important consideration for the personnel expert examining potential sites will be the work stoppage record of that specific location, excluding national strikes. Where only local issues are involved, if management and labor have a good history of working together, that's probably far more important than any so-called right-to-work law. Unfortunately, many companies assume that if a state (mostly those in the Southeast and Southwest) has a right-to-work law that the state government has a management rather than a labor tilt. Not so. Basically all the right-to-work law does is prevent compulsory union membership by an individual employee. It does not prohibit the unionization of companies or prevent the union in such plants from representing the total labor force in collective bargaining.

Another factor of importance to the general labor climate is the rights of management, as evidenced in labor contracts in the local area. If management has been able to retain its right to assign people jobs as needed, with little concern for division of work between competing crafts, then the likelihood is that you will have some flexibility in deploying your work force. Such flexibility may have a larger bearing on your ultimate profitability than any other single labor factor.

One more point that the personnel expert needs to examine is the attitude of the state and local government's labor departments where the regulations and rules under which employees work are established. State labor laws vary considerably from state to state and region to region and are sometimes cited as the reason a company relocates from one area to another.

The makeup of the unemployment compensation system in the state should also be studied. During the 1973–1974 recession, a number of unemployment compensation programs exhausted the reserves set aside from employer contributions. As a result, states had to borrow to pay unemployment. If you locate in a state heavily in debt because it could not manage its unemployment fund, you will probably have to pay a surcharge (at least until the state's federal loan has been repaid).

The formula for paying into the unemployment compensation fund varies state by state. Most states, however, have a merit rating system so that companies with a minimum of layoffs pay a smaller premium into the fund and vice versa.

THE TAX EXPERT

Perhaps the most important job for the expert on taxes is to make a reasonably accurate estimate of future taxes at the proposed relocation site. One such estimate would be the possible future cost of the unemployment compensation fund just discussed.

The tax expert should investigate the bonded indebtedness of the state and the local political subdivision. Investigation of the latter should include special assessment districts such as water, park, recreation, transportation, etc., with an attempt to forecast likely future obligations.

A key component of the evaluation process will be a history of the state and local governments' tax incentives for new or expanding industry. As mentioned previously, however, a low corporate tax rate may not be the blessing it first appears. Corporations lured by low-tax areas may find out later to their dismay that: fire protection is essentially nonexistent (and insurance rates reflect it), police protection is minimal (and insurance rates reflect it), highways are poorly maintained (and truck maintenance records reflect it), and schools are either overcrowded or staffed by mediocre teachers who turn out a poor educational product (and the local employees reflect it).

As in the case of labor laws, companies should look beyond the immediate advantages of some kind of tax forgiveness or tax break and realistically assess the long range impact on the plant's profitability.

THE DISTRIBUTION EXPERT

The transportation expert chosen for the relocation team should be someone familiar with all modes of transportation and capable of performing on-site evaluations of those transportation modes critical to the company's profitability.

For example, the availability of scheduled air service may determine how easily employees at the site can travel to other company locations or call on customers. In addition to the frequency of service, other questions might relate to: whether the runways can handle the new generation of aircraft permitting long distance travel with a minimum of plane changes, whether the airport has the proper navigational instruments for all-weather flying, and how frequently the airport has to close because of bad weather.

Air-cargo-shipment capabilities rate high for companies that make high-value items. Does the airport actually provide air cargo transport, or will additional time be required to truck the packages to another air-cargo terminal?

With respect to the availability of common carrier truck service, the proposed site should be within the commercial zone of some metropolitan area so that the company can utilize *all* the common carrier trucking firms that have rights to serve the area. A problem with some rural locations can be that while you may be on an interstate highway that has thousands of motor carriers moving past your facility daily, few of them may be licensed to provide local service. The end result will be that transportation of your raw materials in, and finished product out, will suffer accordingly.

The same principle holds true for rail service. Rural locations often are outside the switching limits of railroads. As a result, companies that build themselves a nice plant in the country with their own rail spur find they are unable to take advantage of reciprocal switching arrangements. Thus, products shipped via a railroad serving the general location but not a specific site will have to be unloaded at a team track and trucked to the plant.

Even where this is not a problem, being located outside the switching limits means that service in and out of the plant will depend on the local train. The frequent result can be that your box car stays at a nearby classification yard for several days before a local train is made up and the box car switched to your plant by the local crew.

Regarding water transportation, not all ports are open year-round. A check of shipping records can verify if a so-called ice-free port is indeed ice-free.

Another item that should be investigated is the depth of the river or harbor. While they may have been dredged at some time in the past, the depth shown on the navigation charts and the current depth may not be the same.

Many ports have a history of poor labor relations. Don't just rely on official records. A discussion with local traffic managers will inform you if the port has a reputation for pilferage, wildcat strikes, and other forms of unauthorized and often illegal work stoppages.

Finally, the transportation expert should examine the movement of people to and from the proposed plant, mindful that potential problems could be brought on by another energy crisis such as the oil embargo of the early 1970s. If the plant depends on a large work force, discussions should be held to ascertain what, if any, public transportation presently serves the site. If no service exists, sometimes the state or local government will consider initiating and subsidizing such service, or you may be able to encourage such service by cooperating with other companies in the area.

DO YOU NEED A CONSULTANT?

A frequent question that comes up is whether a consultant should be hired to evaluate and make recommendations on sites. A number of companies provide such a service. Many have been involved in plant location analysis for many years and do a capable job. Other firms (e.g., engineering firms, commercial-industrial real estate firms, and construction companies) consult as an ancillary service to their major activity.

A company can be reasonably confident that it will be dealing with professionals who have high standards of ethics and honesty if the site selection team avails itself of "Certified Industrial Developers®." CIDs must have both experience and education in economic development. Many are graduates of the Industrial Development Institute at the University of Oklahoma, an annual training program conducted under the auspices of the American Industrial Development Council. CIDs must have eight years of experience and must successfully pass the Certification Board's testing

20

procedures before receiving the CID designation. (For a list of the 350 or so Certified Industrial Developers, write: American Industrial Development Council, 215 Pershing Road, Suite 707, Kansas City, Missouri 64108.)

Other professionals who will provide expert advice and counsel to a site selection team include members of the Society of Industrial Realtors. This elite segment of the real estate industry deals with commercial and industrial properties. Like CIDs they have passed a rather rigorous examination and compiled a great deal of experience over the years in industrial development. (For further information, contact: Society of Industrial Realtors, 925 15th Street, N.W., Washington, D.C. 20005.)

Those who have the responsibility for developing site selection recommendations may also want to consider availing themselves of the information from such organizations as the Industrial Development Research Council (Peachtree Air Terminal, 1954 Airport Road, Atlanta, Georgia 30341). IDRC, a professional organization of corporate facility planners (the people who generally have the responsibility for site selection within companies), meets twice annually to discuss site selection problems. The Council issues a number of books and publications in the field. Among them is the *Site Selection Handbook*, a quarterly that provides detailed checklists on various aspects of relocation.

Some good reasons for hiring an outside consultant have been suggested by Otto P. Geier, Jr., president of Optimax, Inc., a management consulting firm:[1]

1. The sporadic nature of the task may not justify supporting an internal function.

2. Maintaining confidentiality may be of utmost importance either to avoid community or employee public rela-

tions problems or to keep company officials from being the target of real estate sales efforts.

3. A consultant may be less biased than an internal group.

4. The outside consultant is more likely to make important business issues other than real estate considerations a part of the recommendations.

5. A consultant can interrogate at all levels of the client organization to establish the objectives for relocating or expanding—a task that may be more difficult for an insider.

6. More easily than those within a company, the consultant often can bring together and coordinate the talents of other specialists, as in aerial photography, distribution, etc.

The consultant should be retained only when needed and for a definite time period. Also, the client should make sure that the consultant does not have any economic connection with a developer or other business interest that could compromise the analysis. Success depends in part on the client's ability to open up the necessary channels of communication between the consultant and all levels of the company. Even when companies have competent people on their site selection team, many find that having a consultant double-check the conclusions can be a small price to pay when compared with the size of the investment under consideration.

CHECKLIST

There are a number of checklists that have been developed over the years to aid decision makers in selecting the "best" site. The most complete list appears each year in the September issue (Volume 3) of *Site Selection Handbook*. Now numbering about 1100 items, the list is reviewed and updated annually by the editors.

Our favorite list, however, comes from the now defunct publication, *Factory Management and Maintenance*. Part of that list appears at the end of this chapter; other portions appear at the end of several other chapters in this book. We believe the questions posed by the checklist will serve as a review of some of the important points of the individual chapters.

FIG. 2   Site selection checklist. (SOURCE: *Factory Management and Maintenance*, May, 1957, pp. 180+. Reprinted by permission of Morgan-Gampian Publishing Company.)

---

1. Labor History	*Importance*	*Site*

	Importance	*Site*
Does labor force have deep community roots?	☐	☐
Do most workers own their homes?	☐	☐
Is labor force largely transient?	☐	☐
Can you determine prospects of future labor tranquility as evidenced by convenient indexes such as labor turnover or absenteeism?	☐	☐
Has labor history been satisfactory?	☐	☐
Does one union dominate the area?	☐	☐
Does labor group maintain a good reputation for accepting technological change?	☐	☐
Do employees have a good reputation for housekeeping practices and care of equipment?	☐	☐

2. Labor Availability

Have you made a labor-availability survey? Typical factors:	☐	☐
a. Population at last census.		
b. Population density per square mile.		
c. Percent agricultural.		
d. Total employed in manufacturing.		

FIG. 2 (*Continued*)

	Importance	Site
e. Total employed in nonmanufacturing.		
f. Percent men in labor force.		
g. Countywide potential employment.		
h. Unemployed available workers.		
i. Shift willingness.		
j. Distribution of available labor among skilled, semi-skilled, unskilled groups.		
k. For women, average family income and whether basic need exists for supplemental income.		
Do farm areas serve as good labor pool?	☐	☐
Is there a high degree of farm mechanization (which might affect availability)?	☐	☐
Does community have an increasing supply of women seeking industrial jobs?	☐	☐
Can you complement rather than compete with existing industry? (Example: Hire women from families of male employees.)	☐	☐
Will seasonal jobs in nearby resort areas affect labor availability?	☐	☐
Is community subject to other seasonal labor variations?	☐	☐
Does adequate labor pool exist within reasonable radius?	☐	☐
Are young people taking jobs elsewhere?	☐	☐
Would better job opportunities keep them at home?	☐	☐
Is work group well distributed among industrial, commercial, and service activities?	☐	☐

3. Influence of Local Industry on Labor

Have you considered the principal community factors which will affect your proposed wage rates and working conditions? Typical examples:	☐	☐

Importance Site

a. Wage rates, by skills.
b. Working hours.
c. Shift patterns.
d. Hourly or piece rates.
e. Fringe benefits.
f. Degree of competition for skills.
g. Pattern of year-end bonuses.
h. Degree of unionization.
i. Quality of union leadership.
j. Quality of union "followership."
k. Pattern of productivity.
l. Seniority provisions.
m. Layoff provisions.
n. Grievance patterns.
o. Presence of any unusual or radical tendencies
   (by either management or labor). ☐ ☐

Does industrial accident rate for community
compare favorably with national averages? ☐ ☐

Will you be in direct (or indirect) competition with
an industrial pace-setter? ☐ ☐

4. State Taxes

What is existing gross debt of state, as a partial
indication of future revenue needs? ☐ ☐

Is expected trend likely to keep in line with desired
increased quality of services? ☐ ☐

Do state corporate taxes compare favorably with
those of your competitors elsewhere? ☐ ☐

Does state have income taxes on individuals? ☐ ☐

If so, will they attract new employees from other
states? Or keep them away? ☐ ☐

Does state levy property taxes? ☐ ☐

Is there a state sales tax? ☐ ☐

Does state grant permission to deduct Federal
Income Tax? ☐ ☐

FIG. 2 *(Continued)*

	Importance	*Site*
5. Community Financial Picture		
Does community indebtedness present a healthy picture?	☐	☐
Is community tax picture well balanced between residential, industrial and commercial sources?	☐	☐
Is pattern of community expenditures well balanced between needs and income?	☐	☐
Is total community tax picture in line with services received?	☐	☐
Do abnormally low community taxes indicate inferior schools, streets, other services?	☐	☐
Are there sizable amounts of tax-free property which make an impact upon the community tax picture?	☐	☐
Do future building plans of community government subdivisions threaten potential tax increases?	☐	☐
Does community have special taxes? (payroll, personal income, machinery, equipment, inventory sales, franchise, municipality, county, road improvements, sewer improvement, licenses, permits, fees, etc.)	☐	☐
Are community tax inducements offered to prospective industries?	☐	☐
If so, is there evidence that high taxes later will wipe out initial tax advantage?	☐	☐
Are residential tax rates reasonable?	☐	☐
6. Rail Transportation		
Do groupings of major railroad systems take advantage of natural flow of traffic and thus minimize transfers?	☐	☐
Is proposed location on or near the route of new crack merchandise trains?	☐	☐

	Importance	Site

On a rate-blanketing basis are rates to principal
markets satisfactory? □ □

Has pattern of differential freight rate increases
been relatively favorable for your proposed area? □ □

Does railroad give transit or stop-off privileges for
partial loading or unloading en route? □ □

For LCL type of shipping operations, are there
ample freight forwarders or car-loading
companies? □ □

If more than one railroad serves area, do they have
reciprocal switching arrangements? □ □

Are there adequate truck handling facilities at
freight terminals? □ □

Is pick-up and delivery service available? □ □

Which of these principal physical rail
considerations are important? □ □

   a. Branch or main line.
   b. Freight schedules.
   c. Switchings per day.
   d. Yard limits.
   e. Direction of turnout to private siding from
      yard.
   f. Orientation of site to roadbed.
   g. Relative elevation of site and roadbed.
   h. Potential construction difficulties, such as
      culvert, fill, bridge, cut.

Does prospective rail carrier favor the use of
technologically improved equipment for meeting
of shipper's needs? □ □

7. Truck Transportation.

For truck receipt and shipment operations, which
of these factors are important? □ □
   a. Natural traffic flow.
   b. Specific routes.

FIG. 2 (*Continued*)

	Importance	*Site*

c. Schedules.
d. Rates.
e. Transfers.
f. Common, contract, or private carrier.

	Importance	*Site*
Is the site at or near a "trucking gateway" to reduce in-transit times?	☐	☐
Are state laws as to truck size and weight restrictive?	☐	☐
Will minimum weight restrictions by truckers affect you adversely?	☐	☐
Are there good access roads, bridges, and culverts for trucks?	☐	☐
Is the pattern of recent truck freight rate increases reasonable?	☐	☐
Are state gasoline taxes in line with those at alternate sites?	☐	☐
Can you use newest truck shipment techniques, such as "piggy-back" and "fishy-Back"?	☐	☐
Will the new Federal Highway Program help solve trucking problems?	☐	☐

8. Air Transportation

	Importance	*Site*
If your product consists of high-grade commodities or expeditable merchandise, can you ship by air?	☐	☐
Is site near a good airport?	☐	☐
Are rates and schedules of scheduled air lines satisfactory for air shipment?	☐	☐
Are good nonscheduled airlines available?	☐	☐
Are there good air-freight forwarders nearby?	☐	☐
Do needed air feeder lines exist, or promise to exist?	☐	☐
Is airport service convenient for transport of personnel?	☐	☐
Is there helicopter shuttle service, or (if not) can it be set up economically?	☐	☐

	Importance	Site
9. Water Transportation		
Is proximity to inland water transport important?	☐	☐
Is proximity to overseas shipping important?	☐	☐
Does area have an alert and progressive port authority or comparable commission?	☐	☐
Are water transport rates and schedules competitive?	☐	☐
Are port facilities closed down in winter?	☐	☐
Is access to port convenient and economical?	☐	☐
What about proximity to existing piers?	☐	☐
Are construction costs a factor if new piers are needed?	☐	☐
Is ample lighterage available?	☐	☐
Do any special waterway advantages apply? (Example: "Seatrains" for loaded freight cars on ocean-going ships.)	☐	☐
10. Miscellaneous Transportation	☐	☐
Is railway express service available?	☐	☐
Is Air Express Division of Railway Express available?	☐	☐
Are pipelines usable as common carriers for you?	☐	☐
Does prospective community have a desirable level of passenger transportation facilities (rail, bus, air) for serving employees and families, outside salesmen, visitors, etc.?	☐	☐
Is employee transportation within the community adequate for your expected needs (commuter trains, street cars, buses)?	☐	☐
Are there toll roads or toll bridges that will increase transport costs?	☐	☐
Do winter conditions adversely affect transport?	☐	☐
Does community have public or private warehouses available to help out with short-range inventory storage problems?	☐	☐

In utilizing the checklist, the reader may want to assign a weighted value (say 1 to 4) to each item and thus obtain a numerical value for each location under consideration.

NOTES

1. Otto P. Geier, Jr., "Site Selection and the Outsider," *American Industrial Properties Report*, December 1978, pp. 22–23.

FOUR

How States
Advise and Consent

Would you like some free professional help?

Almost every political jurisdiction in the United States waits eagerly to aid you in your location search. Every state has an office of economic development (by whatever name); most are part of the Department of Commerce or the Department of Business and Industry. And most counties and cities of any size have some kind of staffed economic development organization. The latter may take the form of an industrial development department of a Chamber of Commerce, a not-for-profit industrial foundation, or a county, city, or town government office. All such agencies have detailed information on available industrial sites, population trends, labor availability, transportation systems, and other data you might need for comparing one potential location with another.

But public agencies are not the only ones that will welcome you with open arms and load you down with information on possible locations and stand ready to answer your

31

every question. Private companies, particularly utilities and banks, also have a stake in the game. While the motivating force for most public organizations is the job potential and its ability to reduce the unemployment rolls and add new income and new ratables to an area, the private sector has an economic interest: Your facility represents a way for it to expand its business.

A successful relationship with representatives of economic development organizations (particularly at the local level) will often speed up all the permitting processes which must go on after a final location decision has been made. And utilities and other private companies frequently maintain a list of available industrial properties in their districts and can give you a relatively objective viewpoint on the pros and cons of each location. In all cases, discussions are strictly confidential.

YOU'RE NUMBER ONE

The basic rule of thumb when dealing with the public agencies is "Ask and you may receive." Each state has published guidelines for what it will and will not provide, but you should not assume that these are rules cast in iron. The competition among the states for your business is fierce; the same is true county to county and city to city.

Depending on the size of your business, the wooing can take many forms. If the move represents a sizeable number of people and a substantial investment, don't be too surprised if you get a call from the Governor of the state who invites you for the weekend and sends the state's private airplane to pick up you and your family. Of course, while visiting with the Governor, it would only be appropriate to take a flying tour of the state as the Governor expounds to you the state's benefits and the services the state can provide.

While the above (a true case history of the president of a subsidiary of a major company seeking a relocation site) may not materialize in your case, the point is that you have a very attractive commodity to offer—a facility that will buy or lease land; build or lease a building; transfer in and hire employees; require utilities to provide heat, power, water, and communication services; increase the tax base; pay wages; and purchase directly or indirectly numerous supplies and services. A recent study by the Industrial Development Research Council found that the typical new manufacturing plant provides 159 new jobs.[1]

Some companies, of course, keep their relocation or expansion plans secret until at least the state and perhaps even the general area has been decided upon. There are many reasons for this, not the least of which might be a major increase in land costs when the target area gets wind of the company's interest. Another may be a militant union at the old facility which could, at the least, disrupt or stop normal operations and perhaps even endanger other employees or destroy or damage existing facilities. Also, many firms do not wish to be besieged by developers and others from the public or private community who want a chance to present their case.

Whatever the reason, if you elect to conduct your investigation incognito, don't feel that you'll be treated poorly by the public or private agencies we have been discussing. According to state and private officials, it is not uncommon for companies to go to elaborate means to disguise who they are. Some even go as far as to cut the labels out of their suits lest the people they are talking to discover their city of origin.

33

STATE VERSUS STATE

"In New Jersey, concern for your bottom line starts at the top." "Profit is not a dirty word" (Ohio). "We're not giving business the business any more. We're giving it a break" (New York). "When the old corporate tax bite eats away profits, cut out for Texas." "In Philadelphia your dollar buys prime industrial land at 10 percent of its market value." "San Diego is zoned for success."

All such slogans seek to make location decision makers aware of the benefits awaiting them in their new state, county, or city. In May 1976, *Business Week* explored the competition for industry in a special report entitled "The Second War Between the States" and followed it the next month with "A Counterattack in the War Between the States."

"Despite evidence that special inducements such as tax abatement and low-cost loans play only a limited role in determining where businesses will move," reported *Business Week*, "the stage has been set for a rising spiral of government subsidies as companies play off city against city and state against state for the most advantageous terms.

"There is no such thing as an open city or neutral ground in this struggle. In fact, the greatest pressures from locational incentives fall on the nearest neighboring jurisdictions. Neighbor is pitted against neighbor, and the poor end up taking from the poor."[2]

Summing it up, *Business Week* observed: "The second war between the states will take the form of political and economic maneuver. But the conflict can nonetheless be bitter and divisive because it will be a struggle for income, jobs, people and capital."[3] As Table 2 shows, this time around the South and West have been winning handily.

34

TABLE 2   A Regional Comparison of Changes in Population, Real
Personal Income, and Manufacturing
Employment: 1960–1975

	U.S. average	New England	Middle Atlantic	Great Lakes	Plains States	Rocky Mountain	Far West	South- west	South- east
Population	18.4%	16.1%	10.9%	13.1%	8.4%	31.6%	34.2%	29.4%	23.3%
Real personal income	77.5%	65.5%	57.8%	65.1%	70.5%	93.2%	89.7%	105.8%	114.3%
Manufacturing employment	9.2%	−9.0%	−13.7%	3.2%	8.4%	45.6%	19.8%	67.3%	43.3%

SOURCE: *Business Week,* "The Second War Between the States," May 17, 1976.

The sudden migration has surprised government demog-
raphers and others who predict national trends. By the end
of 1975, nine states on the receiving end—Arkansas, Louis-
iana, Mississippi, South Carolina, Arizona, Texas, Utah,
Alaska, and Hawaii—had already exceeded projected populations for 1980. What gives an indication of the speed of the
shift is the fact that the population projection by the U.S.
Department of Commerce's Bureau of Economic Analysis
was made in 1973.

Although the New England, Middle Atlantic, and Great
Plains states and their major cities have been aggressively
counterattacking by improving the investment incentives
offered industry, the North-to-South momentum continues. To quote *Business Week* again,

> As new markets spring up, the region begins to attract a
> broad array of industries—from manufacturing to all of its
> financial, advertising, wholesaling, printing, and other sup-
> port services. . . . Meanwhile, in the slower-growth regions,
> a declining tax base leads to higher rates of taxation or a cut-
> back in public services. And as people and companies recog-
> nize this, the rush to move out intensifies.[4]

What the location decision maker needs to recognize is
that the new migration of people and industry will have a

strong impact on various aspects of our society. The major cities of the Northeast and Midwest will continue to encounter recurrent fiscal difficulties. And while the South will enjoy the benefits of new ratables for a while, the wage differential between North and South has been closing rapidly and unions have been intensifying their organizing efforts. One Department of Commerce official believes the gap could be virtually closed by 1985. Another economic shift contributing to the migration from the North to South, suggest some, is that from manufacturing to services. As the manufacturing industries have become automated, service jobs have increased, with the result that nearly two-thirds of the United States' private-sector employees work for service companies. Unlike manufacturing companies that have raw material and transportation needs, many service companies can choose to go where it is cheaper to live and, depending on personal tastes, perhaps even better.

One program that has angered the states that have been losing jobs and workers has been the flow of federal funds for public projects. Generally speaking, in recent years the states that constitute New England, the Middle Atlantic region, the Great Lakes, and the Plains have been net losers, while those of the Southeast, Southwest, Rocky Mountain, and Far West regions have been net gainers. Northern states feel that such expenditures may have been justified when the South and West still lagged behind other regions but that the tide has changed. Such funds have been reserved for huge irrigation projects and dams, highway systems, and navigable rivers and streams.

Now, a new federal program has the South crying foul. During the second quarter of 1978, the first $150 million of quarterly awards was made under the Department of Housing and Urban Development's new Urban Development

Action Grant (UDAG) program. The action grant program is the first to express the cornerstone of President Carter's new urban policy—the public-private partnership deemed vital to urban redevelopment. Most of the action grants went toward land acquisition, site clearance, street and infrastructure improvements, demolition and relocation, and loans, second mortgages, and second trusts.

According to *The American City & County:*

> A clear favorite at HUD (the Department of Housing and Urban Development) is a project in Pawtucket, Rhode Island, that will involve buying the old Narragansett race-track. The city will build roads there, install utilities and then sell parcels to private developers. A 45–acre commercial project has already been pledged, as has a 200 unit residential one. Pawtucket has $42 million of private money, a $5.9–million action grant, and $425,000 in block grant money. And, with all that, the city expects to create 3,870 new permanent jobs and add about $2.4 million in property tax revenues.[5]

Business-oriented projects have been slated for about one-third of the dollars under the UDAG program. Companies considering expansion should not write off the urban city option from consideration. Federal and state funds may subsidize such a program for many years to come and could make economic as well as social sense.

HOW A STATE CAN HELP

In addition to the financing programs that will be discussed in detail in Chapter Six, states provide a number of services and can help a search committee narrow its choices. While the Southern states once offered many more investment incentives than the typical Northern state or those of the

Far West, times have changed and the packages available today from one state differ little from another. Figure 3 lists the types of investment incentives that a state, county, or city may provide. *Site Selection Handbook* publishes an annual update of each state's programs.

One financial incentive most states (or counties) offer,

FIG. 3 Possible investment incentives available from the state, county, or city. (SOURCE: U.S. Department of Commerce.)

Financial Help

Industrial revenue bonds
General obligation bonds
Private development credit
Loans for building construction
Loans for machinery and equipment
Incentives for investments in high unemployment areas
Plant expansion assistance
Guarantees for machinery and equipment loans
Guarantees for building construction loans
Free land for industry
State matching funds for local industrial financing programs
State/city/county-owned industrial parks
University R&D available to industry
Employee training/retraining programs

Tax Programs

Corporate tax exemption
Excise tax exemption
Moratorium or exemption on goods in transit (free port)
Moratorium or exemption on land and capital improvements
Exemption on manufacturer's inventories
Stabilization agreements for specified industries
Exemption on raw materials used in manufacturing
Accelerated depreciation for pollution control and other equipment
Tax credits for the use of specified state products
Sales/use exemption on new equipment, particularly for pollution control
Credits against corporate income tax for pollution control facilities
Personal income tax exemption

---

and the one that probably best serves the needs of both the company and the political jurisdiction, is the industrial revenue bond. By issuing such a bond, a jurisdiction raises funds to purchase an industrial plant on behalf of a company. Tax-exempt, these bonds sell for about 1.5 percentage points less than the corporation would have to pay for an equivalent amount of loan to finance its own construction. Since the subsidy comes from a federal tax exemption on the corporation's interest payments on such bonds, the cost of providing the bond is shared by the United States population at large.

In 1969, however, Congress imposed a $10 million limit on such tax-free issues of bonds, except for pollution control, where there is no limit. The limit was imposed at the urging of Northern states disturbed by what they considered to be the South's predatory use of the industrial revenue bond (IRB). In 1968, seven Southern states accounted for 55 percent of all new IRB issues. Once Congress put the lid on tax-free issues, IRB volume dropped to almost nothing— from $1.6 billion in 1968 to $24 million in 1969. In 1978, the limits were changed to permit up to $10 million, effective January 1, 1979. Under certain conditions, such as a UDAG grant area, the total capital expenditure can be $20 million, half of which can be in industrial revenue bonds.

WHAT MARYLAND PROVIDES

As we have stated, the individual states have more similarities than differences in the financial, tax, and consulting services they offer. Officials of the state of Maryland were interviewed to give readers an understanding of how one state runs its program and the services those seeking an industrial site might expect.

In Maryland, the Department of Economic and Community Development's Division of Business and Industrial Development works with out-of-state industry. Its staff is mostly composed of professional economic developers, and several are specialists in such areas as finance, training programs, and market research.

The likelihood, however, is that your first contact will be over the telephone with one of the state's industrial development officers. This official will attempt to fill out a Prospect Data Sheet (See Figure 4). The purpose of this initial contact from the state's standpoint is to define your location requirements, determine if they can be met, suggest the areas of the state or counties best able to satisfy your needs, and try to get you to come and visit.

As should be clear by this time, industrial development is a highly competitive sales situation. The state officials will want to know your deadline and will work nights and weekends should your needs dictate. The state representatives consider their role as that of a catalyst to bring the company and the community together. Toward that end, the representative will act as your intermediary with target communities should you desire to stay anonymous. You can rest assured that your identity will be protected until you are ready to have it revealed.

Confidential discussions can be arranged with plant managers in the area to discuss wage rates, labor characteristics, and other matters that may be of importance. And when you are ready, again incognito or identified, you will be put in touch with the local county or city industrial development professional.

Normally, says one high state official, the company will at least identify itself the second time it elects to visit a community. At that point, the state takes a back seat and the local representative becomes the contact. If a company

FIG. 4 Prospect data sheet. (SOURCE: Division of Business and Industrial Development, Department of Economic and Community Development, State of Maryland.)

Name of Company _____ Date _____

Address _____

Contact _____ Phone _____

Source of Inquiry

Magazine _____ Issue Date _____

Referral (Who) _____

Other (Phone book, NASDA, etc.) _____

Building

Size _____   New   Existing   Purchase   Lease

Special requirements _____

Possession _____

Site

Requirement (size, etc.) _____

Utilities _____

Transportation

Rail _____

Truck _____

Air _____

Water _____

Community

Metropolitan area (downtown or suburbs), smaller city, town ____

Geographic area preferred _____

Labor

Number of employees _____

Type (skilled, unskilled, men, women) _____

Major occupations _____

Wage rates required _____

begins to lose interest, then, he notes, "we will try to find out why and, if it appears the marriage will not take place, we attempt to shift the company's interest to another community."

In Maryland, the counties play an extremely important role. It is the county that issues industrial revenue bonds. Because of the importance of the county in the site selection process, each has a detailed looseleaf notebook entitled "Community Economic Inventory." Figure 5 shows a partial table of contents of one such notebook.

Each of the items shown has historical data and, when appropriate, projections that could prove useful to the inquirer. For example, under Estimated County Labor Potential numbers are provided for: active unemployment-insurance claimants, those who are unemployed and whose claims have expired, those who are unemployed who have not been claimants for unemployment insurance; the under-employed who shift from low-paying or seasonal jobs, high school graduates expected to enter the labor force annually, residents of the county who commute outside the county to work but who would work in the county if comparable jobs were available, and women not now in the labor force who would enter if jobs were available. The summation of these

FIG. 5 Economic inventory of a typical Maryland county. (SOURCE: *Community Economic Inventory*, Washington County, State of Maryland.)

Geographic characteristics	
Climate	Labor
Population	Labor market area
Economic characteristics	Labor force

Estimated county labor
    potential
Wage rates
Fringe benefits
Unions and work stoppages
Labor force characteristics
Existing Industry
    Manufacturing firms
    Other employers
    Services
Business climate
Industrial parks and sites
Transportation
    Railroads
    Highways
    Truck service
    Market area
    Bus service
    Water transportation
    Air service
Communications
    Postal facilities
    Telephone
    Radio
    Television
    Newspapers
Utilities
    Electricity
    Gas
    Fuels
    Water
    Sewerage
Government and taxes

Type of government
Fiscal data
Taxes
Local laws and regulations
    affecting industry
County services
Planning and zoning
Education
    Public elementary and
        secondary education
    Nonpublic schools
    Higher education
County resources
    Housing
    Hotels and motels
    Health
    Financial institutions
    Libraries
    Shopping centers
    Churches
    Community Improvements
Recreation
    Public and private activities
    Cultural, historical, and
        tourist attractions
    Special events
Natural resources
    Agriculture
    Timber
    Minerals
Appendixes
    Industrial financing
    Industrial training

categories gives the estimated total potential labor force that exists within the county for a prospective employer.

The state of Maryland will pay most, if not all, of the training costs for a new employer. If the instructor comes from outside or inside the company and spends full time at the task, for a reasonable period of time, the State will pay the fee or the salary. In addition, it will pick up the tab for training aids, video tape (if the tape is of comparable operations elsewhere), and the portion of utility costs related to the training effort. If training needs to take place while a plant is under construction, the State will arrange for space in a school or other public institution or even rent space. Under special conditions, the State will even pay for the materials consumed in the training operation (for example, metal for a machining or other trade function).

Because the program utilizes only State money, the response to a company's need can be quick and flexible. In some instances, the State will pay for the training elsewhere. One such case involved a British firm that wanted to train six of its potential sixty or so members of the work force as foremen, but the training required a trip to the company's plant in England with room and board for about three months. The state of Maryland provided the funds. Thus, for an expenditure of about $8,000 jobs were provided for 50 or so residents of the State. (Discussion of Maryland's financial assistance options will be treated in detail in Chapter Eight.)

MARYLAND'S PITCH

Each state has its own special attractions and the job of the individual economic development officers includes stressing those features that distinguish it from the competition. For Maryland, the competition comes chiefly from the other states classified by the U.S. Department of Commerce as the Mid-East. In addition to Maryland this includes New York, New Jersey, Pennsylvania (eastern half) and Delaware. Occasionally, Connecticut, Virginia, North Carolina and West Virginia enter the fray. Because of its government laboratories, Maryland has generally been favored over Virginia by the scientific community in the Washington area.

Being the farthest south of its normal competition offers Maryland some advantages. But the key points that are stressed by state officials usually include: proximity to the center of government (Washington, D.C.) and to markets up and down the Eastern seaboard; excellent interstate highways, railroads, water, and air transportation systems; diversity of the labor market; moderate cost of land; and wide choices of community life.

Since the Port of Baltimore is the farthest west of any East Coast port, inland freight costs may be lower. Also, by comparison, the wage and fringe benefits paid the typical Maryland worker usually rank lower than those of states to the north. Moreover, the union influence is not as pervasive as in the North or Midwest and the state has a record of fewer work days lost to strikes and of amenable labor leaders.

And, when compared with costs in other Middle Atlantic states, the cost of land, buildings and other construction tends to be lower.

As in many states, however, different sections of Maryland have their own character. The Cumberland area contains a number of heavy industries, the Eastern Shore region is predominately agricultural with mostly assembly-type industry, and the Washington-Baltimore corridor contains a number of warehouse and distribution facilities plus numerous science-oriented, high-technology companies that draw much of their income from government contracts.

FIG. 6 Site selection checklist. (SOURCE: *Factory Management and Maintenance*, May 1957, pp. 180+. Reprinted by permission of Morgan-Gampian Company.)

11. State Business Climate	*Importance*	*Site*
Are state legislative, executive, and judiciary branches performing as well as or better than counterparts in other states?	☐	☐
Does state have a good reputation regarding attitudes towards industry?	☐	☐
Are state salaries attractive enough to get and keep good people?	☐	☐
Are state officials alert to improving its reputation towards industry?	☐	☐
Are state wage and hours laws fairly written and administered?	☐	☐
Is state workmen's compensation picture satisfactory?	☐	☐
Is state unemployment compensation picture an equitable one?	☐	☐
Does state have laws restricting the use of injunctions to prevent unreasonable union acts?	☐	☐
Does the state have a law that prohibits secondary boycotts?	☐	☐
Do state courts have a progressive viewpoint towards illegal strikes and picketing?	☐	☐
Has history been satisfactory regarding state protection in law enforcement when required locally?	☐	☐
Have you checked with other industries to determine presence of hidden restrictive state laws?	☐	☐
Does state have an active and progressive development commission?	☐	☐

NOTES

1. "New IDRC Research Report Probes Facility Planning Factors," reproduced from *Industrial Development*, May/June 1978, pp. 32–33, by permission of the publishers, Conway Publications, Inc., Atlanta, Georgia. No further reproduction is permitted.

2. "A Counterattack in the War Between the States," *Business Week*, June 21, 1976, pp. 71–74.

3. "The Second War Between the States," *Business Week*, May 17, 1976, pp. 92–111.

4. "The Second War Between the States," op. cit., p. 92.

5. "Federal 'Fund Targeting' Stirs Loser Anger," *The American City and County*, June 1978.

FIVE

Sizing Up
the Locales

While geographic location may not be of major importance to a service company, it can be to producers of goods. Some industrial location specialists believe as much as 10 percent of plant operating costs can be saved annually by the proper geographical choice.

But it is easy to make mistakes, too, by working from yesterday's knowledge. For example, the Northwest no longer has its huge surplus of power since the severe droughts of 1976 to 1977 forced plants to shift from hydroelectric to other forms, with the attendant increased cost being borne by the customer. Now, however, oil from Alaska could create a new center of industry along the Pacific Coast of Oregon and Washington.

Similarly, the new efforts to develop oil and gas off the Atlantic Coast could have a profound impact on the economy of such states as New Jersey, Delaware, and Maryland, which have large undeveloped areas along their Eastern shores, and of Long Island. And the New England, Northern, and Midwestern states have been updating their industrial development programs. The major cities in these areas, too, have recognized that some changes have to be made, and innovative programs have been planned and in some instances at least partially implemented. In Hartford, Connecticut, an in-depth development plan for that city has resulted in renewal of part of the downtown and attraction of some new industry. And in New York, politicians have been talking about creating a tax haven district in the South Bronx.

All of which means that the location decision maker should start with an open mind so that all options can be uncovered for consideration.

The first rule is to "know thyself." That means breaking down current costs into component parts. Figure 7 suggests

FIG. 7 Worksheet for comparing the cost of present and proposed facilities. (SOURCE: Developed by the author.)

		Old	New
Transportation:			
Raw material costs		___	___
Freight charges		___	___
Warehousing		___	___
	Subtotal	___	___
Manufacturing Improvements:			
Process changes		___	___
Economies of scale		___	___
	Subtotal	___	___
Labor:			
Labor, wages		___	___
Labor, benefits		___	___
Training costs		___	___
Automation		___	___
Productivity gains			___
Shift differentials		___	___
	Subtotal	___	___

Utilities:		Old	New
Power		___	___
Fuel		___	___
Water		___	___
	Subtotal	___	___
Environment:			
Sewage treatment		___	___
Waste water treatment		___	___
Air pollution control		___	___
OSHA* related costs		___	___
	Subtotal	___	___
Marketing:			
Quality control improvements		___	___
Average cost of sales call		___	___
Change in product mix		___	___
Inventory requirements		___	___
	Subtotal	___	___
Administrative Costs:			
Local real estate taxes		___	___
Other local taxes		___	___
State taxes		___	___
Unemployment insurance		___	___
Other taxes (sewage, etc.)		___	___
Rent/lease charges		___	___
Depreciation/interest		___	___
Maintenance charges		___	___
	Subtotal	___	___
Miscellaneous:			
Cost peculiar to location		___	___
Work flow changes		___	___
Executive productivity and other intangibles		___	___
	Subtotal	___	___
Estimated Total of Old vs. New		___	___

*Occupational Safety & Health Administration.

one form for the calculation. We have included several items under *Miscellaneous* which are often overlooked which will require a subjective rather than objective evaluation.

It's important to keep in mind throughout the location-decision-analysis process that any move of whatever distance provides the perfect opportunity to ask whether any step of the manufacturing, marketing, or administrative functions can be improved or eliminated. Can you cut down the number of manufacturing operations? Can you automate? Use a different process? Solve a pollution problem? Provide for future expansion? Develop a new market? Serve an old market better?

The questions can go on and on and are unique to each situation. The point, however, is that until you know the problems of the old location you just can't make a rational decision on either what the new facility should do for the company or where it should be built or bought. Then, depending on whether you are moving a "product" or a "people" factory, Figure 7 takes on meaning.

For a people factory, the quality of life can be an important aspect for improving such intangibles as executive productivity. On the other hand, studies have shown that when low-level workers have to drive through and work in communities way beyond their means their productivity suffers. As for driving times, a rule of thumb: hourly workers won't ordinarily drive more than thirty minutes to work, and forty-five minutes approaches the limit for higher-paying jobs.

In addition to measuring each location in terms of economic goals and objectives and studying the plant operating requirements so that the ability of the local community to respond can be evaluated, the rivalry factor must be considered. Community members, whether they are antagonistic (other producers of the product) or cooperative (customers or resource suppliers), can be expected to react to a decision maker's locational choice. Competitors may counter the decision maker's action with a retaliatory response. The decision maker who is knowledgeable about the extent of rivalry will make a choice of location that anticipates the response of rivals, weighing the likelihood of such a response to determine the expected payoff of any location. Of course, the new plant will change the distance from the customer and the supplier, which will in turn reduce or increase costs.

Only when the pricing and marketing strategies have been established can the decision maker concentrate on maximizing the rate of return on plant investment. The best rate of return will be achieved by finding one or more least-cost plant sites and then weighing the tangibles and intangibles against one another, keeping in mind the fact that the facility will have to attract and keep good people.

LOCATION THEORY

While retail and commercial locations depend upon population and markets, the location of industrial plants is much more complex. Back in 1875, Johann Heinrich von Thunen studied agricultural location and reasoned that the heaviest and least valuable agricultural product should be raised close to the city. Further, if two farmers produce the same product and sell it for the same price the one closest to the city can spend more for machinery, labor, fertilizer, etc.

In 1909, Alfred Weber expanded on von Thunen's use of transportation costs as a basis for industrial location. Weber classified resources into those available everywhere (air and water) and *localized materials*, those limited to certain locations (minerals, ores, etc.). From the manufacturing stand-point, he called those that lost no weight in processing *pure materials* and materials like ores *weight-losing*. Weber's consequent location theory was relatively simple, but it does help to explain many contemporary practices.

Here are some examples: The juice is removed from oranges and the water eliminated close to the orange groves and then shipped to the rest of the country as orange juice concentrate. The consumer buys the concentrate and adds the water without having to pay for the cost of transporting it. An orange drink sold at the grocery store will usually be produced nearby. Similarly, for bottled or canned soft drinks, the syrup from which they are made will normally be sent to the bottling plant where the water is added. In metal manufacturing, fuel is a major ingredient in smelting. The decision must be made whether to ship the ore to the fuel or the fuel to the ore. When several raw materials are used, an intermediate location may be the point of least transfer cost.

As viewed by Weber, industry divides itself into two groups: those oriented to labor and those oriented to transportation. When two alternative locations come out about equal on these two counts, then consideration of *agglomeration factors* becomes important. *Agglomeration factors* refers to closeness to suppliers, economics of size, improved marketing outlets, etc.

In 1948, Edgar M. Hoover separated the cost factors of location into (1) transportation factors and (2) production factors. Transportation was defined as the cost of procuring the raw materials and distributing the finished product. Production included not only labor and other manufacturing costs but also the agglomerative and institutional forces. He stressed that terminating costs are independent of the length of haul and that the cost per mile of the haul decreases with distance. Thus, water transport, with high terminal costs, usually involves long-distance shipments. Hoover included in agglomeration such advantages as better transfer services, a broader, more flexible labor market, more advanced banking facilities, better police and fire protection, and lower insurance costs and utility rates.

A problem with these theoretical approaches is that they presuppose a unique location that has a site equally advantageous for serving all areas of the market. In real life, a location may be the most profitable despite the fact that it has a high cost relative to other locations or to the market area. Market area in locational theory does not refer to the number of square miles but to dollar volume of sales. Thus, a freight or production cost disadvantage narrows the market area; conversely, an advantage widens the market area. Marvin L. Greenhut observes of those attempting to derive a least-cost location:

> Any producer . . . must choose first among buying centers. The determination of the best cosumption points (area) involves the concept of demand; or otherwise expressed, it is the location of competitors which predetermines price and sales at any buying point for any firm. . . . Location in the backyard of rivals is therefore self-explained; more customers or the same number of customers . . . can be served at price "P" and cost "X" than is possible from any other location . . . selection of a site calls forth not only substitution among costs at alternative locations, but a balancing of all factors accounting for profit, demand, and cost.[1]

The purpose of these and other location exercises lies in getting the searcher to be divorced from personal preferences and able to calculate the financial benefits of alternative sites. When making such comparisons, choose one as a reference point, and then compare the relative costs of sales, transportation, etc., of other options.

A recent study[2] tested a number of hypotheses dealing with the importance of labor, markets, materials (including transport costs), return on capital, and residual factors (tax-cost considerations, etc.) in regional location decisions. The conclusion was that the greatest significance continues to be placed on labor and markets, with the aim of maximizing productivity and profits.

GOVERNING FACTORS

Deciding *why* the company should relocate or expand precedes the decision of where. In 1977, the Market Research Department of *The Wall Street Journal* analyzed the results of 1200 questionnaires designed to ascertain corporate intentions to relocate, acquire, or build new or additional facilities. The survey found, among other things, that about half the companies were planning expansion moves within the next two years: 76 percent planned a manufacturing plant, 59 percent a distribution center, 51 percent a regional or divisional office, 33 percent a research and development facility, and 34 percent a corporate headquarters. On the average, the companies expected to take about nine months from initial investigation to final selection of a facility or site[3].

Figure 8 provides an excerpt from the questionnaire. The reader should answer the questions in Figure 8 and then compare the answers with those in Table 3 which summarizes the survey results.

A study of Table 3 yields some interesting conclusions.

FIG. 8 Relative importance of several factors in facility location decisions. (SOURCE: *Business on the Move*, Dow Jones & Co., Inc., Market Research Dept., 1977.)

Type of Facility: _____ Manufacturing Plant

_____ Distribution Center

_____ Regional/Divisional Office

_____ Research & Development Facility

_____ Corporate Headquarters

_____ Other (Write In) _____

Please circle: 1 if *critical*, would not consider if unavailable
2 if *very important* and marginally critical
3 if *somewhat important*, but not critical
4 if of *slight* or *no* importance.

Availability of labor	1	2	3	1
Tax abatements/incentives	1	2	3	4
Transportation facilities:				
Air	1	2	3	4
Highway	1	2	3	4
Rail	1	2	3	4
Water	1	2	3	4
Availability of raw materials	1	2	3	4
Accessibility to markets:				
Established	1	2	3	4
New	1	2	3	4
Availability of financing	1	2	3	4
Large land area	1	2	3	4
"Right to Work" laws	1	2	3	4
Availability of executive/professional talent	1	2	3	4
Availability of energy/fuel	1	2	3	4

TABLE 3 Importance of 14 Major Relocation Factors by Type of Facility

	All company facilities Rank	%*	Manufacturing plant Rank	%*	Distribution center Rank	%*	Regional divisional office Rank	%*	R&D facility Rank	%*	Corporate headquarters Rank	%*
Availability of labor	1	93	1	79	4	43	6	31	4	18	5	18
Tax abatements/incentives	12	56	10	49	9	33	9	20	8	13	6	17
Transportation facilities												
Air	7	64	13	41	7	34	1	38	2	20	1	26
Highway	3	90	3	75	1	60	2	37	3	19	2	24
Rail	6	66	6	59	6	43	13	14	14	8	12	10
Water	14	39	14	34	14	23	14	13	13	8	13	9
Availability of raw materials	8	63	5	61	13	23	12	14	12	11	14	8
Accessibility to markets												
Established	4	85	4	65	2	58	4	33	10	11	10	13
New	5	77	7	55	3	53	5	31	11	11	11	12
Availability of financing	13	51	12	46	11	31	10	20	9	13	7	16
Large land area	9	63	9	53	10	32	11	18	6	13	8	14
'Right to work" laws	11	58	8	54	8	34	8	20	7	13	9	14
Availability of executive/professional talent	10	62	11	46	12	29	3	34	1	22	3	22
Availability of energy/fuel	2	91	2	78	5	43	7	29	5	18	4	20

*Weighted Response. On a four-point scale: a critical rating (1) by a respondent received 100%; a very important rating (2) received 75%; a shomewhat important rating (3) received 25%; and a slight or of no-importance rating (4) received 0%. Thus, if all respondents rated an item 2, it would have a 75% weighted response.

SOURCE: "Business on the Move," Dow Jones & Co., Inc., Market Research Dept., 1977.

On a weighted response basis,* almost all of these factors are at least somewhat important for a manufacturing plant. While less critical for a distribution center, still all of the factors except raw materials availability and water transportation facilities would be considered at least somewhat important.

When the analysis moves from product to people factories, the significance of individual factors drops off dramatically with the two most important—air and highway transportation facilities—achieving a weighted response of less than 40 percent. For corporate headquarters, air transportation tops the list with only a 26 percent weighted average. For the R&D facility, the availability of executive or professional talent only brought a 22 percent weighted response.

What this clearly shows is that people factories have a lot more flexibility in the choice of location than do those that make or distribute product.

Now that you have some idea of what factor or factors are of most concern to you, the question of where can be addressed. An interesting input in the search might be an awareness of what development organizations in the various states would rank as their key economic assets. Table 4 provides such a listing. The data was developed by Conway Publications, publishers of *Industrial Development* and *Site Selection Handbook*, from a questionnaire distributed to several thousand development organizations that were asked to rank eight locational factors from one to eight, with one being the most important.

---

*To obtain a weighted response: a *critical* rating of 1 received 100%; a *very important* rating, or 2, received 75%; a *somewhat important*, or 3, received 25%; a *slight or of no importance* rating of 4 received 0%. Thus, if all respondents rated an item 2, it would have a 75% weighted response.

TABLE 4   The Relative Importance of Plant
Location Factors

	Labor availability	Resource availability	Energy availability	Transportation	Taxes on business and industry	Availability of land	Lack of red tape in obtaining environmental permits	Quality of life
Alabama	①	2	3	4	5	6	8	7
Alaska	Insufficient response to permit tally.							
Arizona	①	8	5	7	3	4	6	2
Arkansas	①	6	3	4	2	5	8	7
California	①	5	4	8	6	3	7	2
Colorado	①	3	6	4	7	5	8	2
Connecticut	①	6	7	4	5	3	8	2
Delaware	①	8	6	5	4	2	7	3
Florida	①	8	6	4	5	2	7	3
Georgia	①	8	5	4	6	2	7	3
Hawaii	①	7	5	6	4	3	8	2
Idaho	①	7	6	3	4	5	8	2
Illinois	2	5	6	①	7	3	8	4
Indiana	①	5	4	2	7	6	8	3
Iowa	①	6	4	5	7	2	8	3
Kansas	3	7	5	5	6	2	8	4
Kentucky	①	7	2	3	6	5	8	4
Louisiana	①	4	2	5	6	3	7	8
Maine	①	6	3	7	5	2	8	4
Maryland	2	7	6	①	5	4	8	3
Massachusetts	3	6	7	4	8	2	5	①
Michigan	①	7	4	5	6	3	8	2
Minnesota	①	4	2	3	7	6	8	5
Mississippi	①	7	4	5	3	2	8	6
Missouri	①	6	2	4	5	3	8	7
Montana	2	①	3	8	6	4	7	5
Nebraska	①	8	4	2	6	5	7	3

	Labor availability	Resource availability	Energy availability	Transportation	Taxes on business and industry	Availability of land	Lack of red tape in obtaining environmental permits	Quality of life
Nevada	6	7	5	3	①	4	8	2
New Hampshire	2	8	7	①	3	4	5	6
New Jersey	①	8	4	3	6	2	7	5
New Mexico	2	6	①	7	3	4	8	5
New York	①	7	5	2	6	3	8	4
North Carolina	①	7	6	3	5	4	8	2
North Dakota	5	①	2	6	7	4	8	3
Ohio	①	7	5	2	6	3	8	4
Oklahoma	2	5	①	3	4	6	8	7
Oregon	①	4	3	5	8	6	7	2
Pennsylvania	①	5	6	3	7	2	8	4
Rhode Island	①	3	4	5	6	7	8	2
South Carolina	3	8	①	5	4	2	7	6
South Dakota	2	5	7	6	①	4	8	3
Tennessee	①	6	3	2	7	5	8	4
Texas	①	7	2	6	4	3	8	5
Utah	2	3	①	5	6	7	8	4
Vermont	2	7	4	5	6	3	8	①
Virginia	①	7	6	3	4	2	8	5
Washington	①	7	2	5	6	4	8	3
West Virginia	2	3	①	4	7	5	8	6
Wisconsin	①	7	4	5	6	2	8	3
Wyoming	7	4	3	5	①	2	8	6

SOURCE: "Rapid Geo-Economic Changes Pose Elusive Targets for Facility Planners," *Site Selection Handbook*, May 1978, pp. 82–83. (Reproduced by permission of Conway Publications, Inc., Atlanta, Georgia.)

TABLE 5   Key Economic Data by States and Regions

States and regions	Population		Income				Employees, Earnings and Hours of Work						
	Population (000s), July 1, 1975	Population projection (000s), 1990	Personal income (billions), 1975	Percent change 1974-1975	Per capita personal income (I), 1975	Personal income, percent increase, 1969-1990	Employees in nonagricultural establishments (000s), 1975	Union membership as percent of nonagricultural employment, 1972	Unemployment, percent of persons 16 years old and over, May 1976	Manufacturing establishments, 1972	Manufacturing, employees (000s), 1975	Manufacturing, production workers average hourly earnings (I), 1975	Manufacturing, production workers average weekly earnings (I), 1975
United States	213,121	250,630	1,243.3	8.0	5,834	119	76,868	27.2	7.3	320,710	18,146	4.35	172.70
New England	12,198	14,656	74.2	7.2	6,086	117	4,699	—	—	23,732	1,312	—	—
Maine	1,059	1,220	5.1	5.4	4,785	92	356	19.1	7.3	2,076	96	3.81	152.02
New Hampshire	8.8	900	4.3	6.6	5,210	136	293	17.2	4.2	1,434	85	3.95	154.05
Vermont	471	549	2.3	8.8	4,925	129	159	17.7	9.0	860	39	4.07	164.43
Massachusetts	5,828	7,054	35.9	7.5	6,159	120	2,328	26.0	8.0	10,770	594	4.47	174.78
Rhode Island	927	1,168	5.5	9.6	5,917	116	343	27.3	9.5	2,756	109	3.84	149.04
Connecticut	3,095	3,774	21.2	6.4	6,854	112	1,220	26.1	9.1	5,836	389	4.78	193.59
Mideast	42,656	50,583	273.5	7.3	6,411	110	16,104	—	—	76,517	3,791	—	—
New York	18,120	23,147	119.7	7.3	6,603	102	6,791	36.2	8.9	38,341	1,407	4.91	191.00
New Jersey	7,316	8,694	48.5	5.8	6,629	122	2,668	29.1	9.2	15,069	736	4.93	199.99
Pennsylvania	11,827	13,234	69.5	7.8	5,874	108	4,416	38.2	7.6	18,398	1,336	4.96	190.96
Delaware	579	687	3.9	9.0	6,799	127	1,227	20.3	7.6	567	67	5.07	200.27
Maryland	4.098	4,821	26.4	8.4	6,437	145	1,424	21.7	5.8	3,579	230	5.03	196.67
District of Columbia	716	—	5.5	8.3	7,751	85	578	—	7.2	563	15	5.52	212.52
Great Lakes	40,979	49,602	251.3	7.3	6,131	110	15,162	—	—	64,674	4,505	—	—
Michigan	9,157	11,197	57.1	6.8	6,240	109	3,127	38.4	9.7	14,467	980	6.15	250.76
Ohio	10,759	12,838	63.3	6.9	5,883	111	4,010	34.8	6.8	16,390	1.258	5.55	223.67
Indiana	5,311	6,354	29.7	7.3	5,587	117	1,930	33.9	N/A	7,354	544	5.49	218.50
Illinois	11,145	13,729	75.2	7.7	6,750	108	4,425	35.6	6.7	18,618	1,220	5.40	214.50
Wisconsin	4,607	5,484	25.9	8.2	5,627	109	1,670	29.7	5.4	7,845	503	5.26	212.25
Plains	16,690	19,668	95.4	8.7	5,715	105	5,939	—	—	21,467	1,224	—	—
Minnesota	3,926	4,797	13.5	6.4	5.754	127	1,470	28.3	4.8	5,698	313	5.10	200.43
Iowa	2,870	3,376	16.9	12.3	5,899	95	993	20.0	4.5	3,387	230	5.40	214.38
Missouri	4,763	5,410	22.6	6.7	5,387	114	1,719	32.9	4.8	6,732	400	4.75	185.25
North Dakota	635	797	3.7	4.5	5,855	69	197	16.1	4.4	482	15	4.32	171.07
South Dakota	683	844	3.4	6.4	4,980	83	209	11.8	3.8	606	20	4.20	172.20
Nebraska	1,546	1,804	9.5	17.2	6,175	92	554	17.0	4.3	1,723	85	4.51	183.68
Kansas	2,267	2,640	13.5	8.4	5,968	85	797	15.4	3.6	2,839	161	4.65	189.98
Southeast	47,773	52,775	235.3	6.7	4,926	146	15,919	—	—	59,905	3,904	—	—
Virginia	4,967	5,603	28.2	7.6	5,671	149	1,755	15.5	5.0	4,837	366	3.99	156.41
West Virginia	1,803	1,761	8.7	10.9	4,815	104	561	41.3	5.4	1,734	120	4.90	190.12

States and regions	Population (000s), July 1, 1975	Population projection (000s), 1990	Personal income (billions), 1975	Percent change 1974-1975	Per capita personal income (l), 1975	Personal income, percent increase, 1969-1990	Employees in nonagricultural establishments (000s), 1975	Union membership as percent of nonagricultural employment, 1972	Unemployment, percent of persons 16 years old and over, May 1976	Manufacturing establishments, 1972	Manufacturing, employees (000s), 1975	Manufacturing, production workers average hourly earnings (l), 1975	Manufacturing, production workers average weekly earnings (l), 1975
Kentucky	3,396	3,854	15.9	6.3	4,668	139	1,042	24.9	5.6	3,167	254	4.65	180.42
Tennessee	4,188	4,575	20.0	6.2	4,766	149	1,497	18.4	7.3	5,647	454	3.92	156.02
North Carolina	5,451	6,075	26.2	5.7	4,801	139	1,996	7.5	5.8	8,632	737	3.51	135.14
South Carolina	2,818	3,206	12.7	6.1	4,521	132	978	9.0	5.8	3,719	336	3.59	141.45
Georgia	4,926	5,698	24.5	5.5	4,969	142	1,725	13.9	N/A	7,629	433	3.88	152.10
Florida	8,357	7,805	46.1	5.3	5,517	203	2,729	14.7	9.9	10,275	328	4.04	160.39
Alabama	3,614	4,126	16.5	9.2	4,557	127	1,150	19.2	6.6	4,984	320	4.13	163.55
Mississippi	2,346	2,832	9.5	7.3	1,011	122	667	12.6	3.3	2,727	198	3.55	139.52
Louisiana	3,791	4,711	17.9	8.4	4,729	105	1,199	16.9	7.5	3,657	182	4.81	197.69
Arkansas	2,116	2,329	9.3	7.1	4,383	131	620	16.4	5.4	2,897	176	3.59	139.29
Southwest	18,320	21,300	96.56	9.8	5,265	131	6,388	—	—	20,429	1,075	—	—
Oklahoma	2,712	2,941	13.5	9.1	4,996	120	887	16.0	7.4	3,042	150	4.41	176.84
Texas	12,237	14,514	65.9	10.4	5,387	127	4,413	13.5	N/A	14,424	800	4.57	185.54
New Mexico	1,147	1,470	5.1	10.7	4,482	113	364	13.2	6.1	926	27	3.67	143.50
Arizona	2,224	2,375	11.9	7.2	5,329	177	724	16.6	N/A	2,037	98	4.85	189.15
Rocky Mountain	5,682	6,436	31.0	8.6	5,452	126	2,037	—	—	6,709	281	—	—
Montana	748	873	4.1	11.6	5,434	80	240	30.7	6.0	943	22	5.32	195.78
Idaho	820	907	4.1	3.9	4,980	98	268	17.0	N/A	1,190	47	4.72	183.61
Wyoming	374	417	2.2	14.5	5,942	87	143	18.5	3.5	377	8	5.11	205.07
Colorado	2,534	2,730	14.8	7.5	5,839	147	948	18.9	N/A	2,841	135	4.58	183.66
Utah	1,206	1,509	5.8	10.9	4,819	139	438	19.4	5.7	1,358	69	4.05	155.52
Far West	28,826	37,636	177.6	10.9	6,434	117	10,620	—	—	47,276	2,054	—	—
Washington	3,544	4,116	22.1	11.1	6,226	98	1,209	38.3	8.3	5,345	242	5.79	224.07
Oregon	2,288	2,425	12.8	7.2	5,610	121	831	27.9	9.0	4,670	182	5.54	212.74
Nevada	592	629	3.9	11.7	6,524	168	264	33.6	8.0	447	12	5.26	200.93
California	21,185	28,851	138.9	10.1	6,555	119	7,815	28.9	9.6	35,703	1,585	5.21	205.80
Alaska	352	449	3.1	33.6	8,815	134	162	27.6	9.7	341	9	6.70	261.97
Hawaii	865	1,166	5.5	8.1	6,426	135	339	37.0	8.5	770	24	4.62	181.10
Outlying U.S. Area	3,034	—	—	—	—	—	779	—	—	2,437	155	—	—
Puerto Rico	2,951	—	5.7	—	2,204	—	770	20.0	—	2,340	152	—	—
Virgin Islands	83	—	—	—	—	—	9	—	—	97	3	—	—

SOURCE: U.S. Department of Commerce, Bureau of International Commerce.

As can be observed, labor availability rated top mention for most states. Montana and North Dakota chose resource availability. Five states listed energy availability as of first importance—New Mexico, Oklahoma, South Carolina, Utah, and West Virginia. Illinois, Maryland, and New Hampshire pointed to transportation as their key asset. Policies regarding taxes on business and industry were listed number 1 by Nevada, South Dakota, and Wyoming. And Massachusetts and Vermont thought their best attribute was quality of life.

A number of other statistics may become important to the locational decision maker at this point. The historical reservoir of such data continues to be the U.S. Department of Commerce. As of September 1978, the latest statistical profile of the United States had just been issued. Last published in 1972 and updated every five years, *The County and City Data Book 1977* contains many facts about: 3000 counties; 910 incorporated cities of 25,000 or more inhabitants; 277 standard metropolitan statistical areas (SMSAs) defined as of June 1977; states and groupings of states; and the 10 standard federal administrative regions and census geographic divisions and regions.

The new volume contains 195 data items for counties and 190 for cities. Included are maps, charts, and 770 pages of tabular material. The tables provide facts on population, income, housing, manufacturers' employment and payrolls, and other subjects of interest to location decision makers. A series of state maps depict counties, metropolitan areas, and cities. Several appendixes provide information on population rank, change in land area for cities, and population data for all places of 2500 or more inhabitants.

Table 5 shows the type of data available in this book and

from government agencies. This particular collection of data was prepared by the U.S. Department of Commerce's Bureau of International Commerce for distribution to potential foreign investors.

NOTES

1. Melvin L. Greenhut, *Plant Location*, The University of North Carolina Press, 1956, pp. 98-100.

2. Richard A. Stanford, *An Analysis of the Empirical Relationships Between Productivity Measures and Regional Industry Location*, Ph.D. dissertation, University of Georgia, 1971.

3. "Business on the Move," Dow Jones & Co., Inc., Market Research Department, 1977.

SIX

Key Industrial Location Factors

Labor, markets, transportation, and energy-fuel availability plus access to raw materials top the list of concerns for manufacturing industries. Also important are utility availability and costs, environmental factors, and climate considerations. The object of the search is to find that location which minimizes cost and maximizes revenues.

LABOR

The labor market for a particular place means the number of workers who can be attracted without changing where they live. As previously noted, hourly workers will rarely drive more than 30 minutes to work and a 45-minute commute approaches the limit for salaried employees.

Workers can be divided into five classes: unskilled, semiskilled, craftsmen and other highly skilled non-professionals, skilled professionals, and executives.

Firms requiring highly skilled labor must normally locate where the highly skilled labor lives. When critical factors dictate another area, skilled workers may have to be brought in to train the local unskilled labor force—a costly and time-consuming process.

The productivity of the local labor force rates first consideration. Advantages of an area that offers low wage rates may be offset by low productivity rates. Conversely, high wages should not repel an employer, since the bottom line may be low production costs. And regardless of the analysis that went before, low labor costs will not be realized if the local labor force proves unstable. High labor turnover is expensive; retraining and lost production are cost factors not easily recovered.

The size of the necessary labor force can also limit location possibilities. Manufacturers who require large work forces normally are restricted to densely populated areas. However, a community with other attractive features should not be eliminated just because at first glance its size does not appear to meet the manpower needs. The *total* manpower reserve may prove more than sufficient when the transportation, commuting, and shopping characteristics of the community are plotted. Also, if the average family income of the area is low, the company may be able to attract large numbers of women into the work force.

Still, the necessity for analyzing the *permanent labor surplus* cannot be overemphasized. Carpenters and other craftsmen may draw unemployment during the winter months, but the high seasonal wages provided by such trades means that they will usually not accept steady industrial employment. Likewise, students and agricultural workers can boost the average labor force as much as 6 percent in the summer.

Thus, while the available supply of labor for a new industry comes from workers who are unemployed, the analysis has to determine why the unemployment rolls are high. Part of the answers can usually be obtained by talking with other employers in the target area. This can also give you an idea of the labor stability of the area and the attitudes of the local labor force and of unions toward the employers, and vice versa. Conversations with local union heads can provide further insights. And the U.S. Bureau of Labor Statistics can furnish data on the number of strikes in the community, and their duration.

For employers of a large work force, the workmen's compensation insurance rates can be a limiting factor when comparing one location against another. These vary substantially among the states and should be checked along with other state labor laws before making a final decision.

MARKETS

While labor is an important influence upon location decisions, it often takes second place to markets and transportation for product-oriented companies.

Several major forces influence transfer costs for particular industries and make the point of least-transfer-cost one close to the source of raw materials. These forces are (1) great loss of weight in raw materials during production or processing, (2) availability of raw materials for mining and other extractive industries, and (3) the perishability of the raw material. Conversely, the beverage industry and others that tend to locate near the market do so because they: (1) add weight (such as water) during the production of finished products, (2) experience large differentials in rates between raw materials and finished products, or (3) produce a highly perishable finished product, e.g., baked goods and ice cream.[1]

One way around the problem is the use of in-transit privileges by companies such as the steel industry where the raw material may be shipped to a production point and then to final destination at a combined cost slightly less than the through rate. A firm that uses several raw materials can usually realize lowest transfer costs by locating at collection points. A collection point, by definition, is one that minimizes the accumulation costs for various materials; a distribution point is a location that has minimum distribution costs to various markets.

Although rates are subject to regulation, the carrier sets them. Another important point: Published rates do not necessarily reflect the rate at which freight actually moves. It is necessary to make a detailed study of the relevant commodities rather than to accept published rates.

Many manufacturers as well as wholesale and retail dealers have overexpanded their market areas. *They ship too far at a loss.* The geographical marginal cost exeeds the marginal revenue. Field sales operations penetrate too far into unprofitable territory. Many small manufacturers have made the error of seeking national distribution at great expense only to find that a greater volume of business at a much smaller cost could be secured within a few miles of the plant.

In striving for sales volume it has been easy to lose sight of the sales expense attached. The worst possible business policy is to canvass outlying areas intensively and absorb the freight costs. It is better not to solicit business in these areas at all and to charge at least half the freight to the customer.

A government study of the confectionary business examines two groups of companies. The results are shown in Table 6. Group I accepted distant sales but did not solicit them; Group II went after distant sales vigorously (as can be

70

TABLE 6   The Relationship between Selling Costs and Distance
All figures represent percentage of total sales

			Selling costs						Profit	
Distance of	Sales by zones		Total		Direct cost		Freight portion			
customer (miles)	I	II	I	II	I	II	I	II	I	II
To 500	82%	81%	23%	36%	8%	10%	2%	2%	2%	2%
500–1000	13	14	25	46	7	14	7	6	3	−3
1000–1500	2	3	16	21	4	8	5	3	3	−5
1500+	3	2	15	25	3	8	5	7	3	−5

SOURCE: August Losch, *The Economics of Location*, Yale University Press, 1954, p. 398.

seen from the selling costs). Profits show that Group I had the right policy.

As a general rule, the ratio of selling costs to sales generally increases with distance. The farther the sales representative is from home or the closer to the competitor, the less likely it is that the sale will transfer down to the bottom line. Another study found that the proportion of accounts overdue tends to be greater among distant customers.

An increasing number of observers believe the future lies in intermodal transportation. "Unfortunately, in the typical metropolitan area today there is little if any coordination of the truck mode, rail mode, rapid transit and air mode systems," observed *Site Selection Handbook* in 1976. The handbook further observed

> Each system was developed with little thought to the intermodal transfer of people or goods. . . . Thus, it is not uncommon for a shipper to discover that in moving goods from his plant or warehouse in City A to a customer's plant or warehouse in City B the greatest cost is not the transportation from Point A to Point B, but the transfer services prior to departure in City A and subsequent to arrival in City B.[2]

71

For such reasons astute planners now look for their major savings on each end of the trip rather than en route. This thinking is focusing new attention on sites such as the hypothetical one shown in Figure 9. While a company may not need the quadramodal super sites shown in Figure 9, it may be looking for a trimodal or bimodal facility. For many shippers the ultimate is a standardized container that can be moved by jumbo jet, by rail, by truck, or by ship with equal ease.

The facility and the transportation modes can be treated as a single system. One large manufacturing company now includes the transportation systems as part of the capital cost

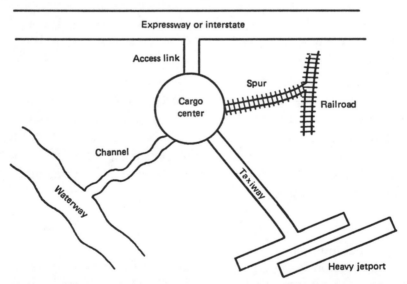

FIG. 9   Typical intermodal cargo center. New intermodal cargo centers will attract industrial plants and distribution facilities for many firms. (SOURCE: "Transportation: The Key Element in Geo-Economic Planning," *Site Selection Handbook*, February 1976, p. 80. Reproduced by permission of Conway Publications, Inc., Atlanta, Georga.)

of a new plant. Thus, the company-owned vehicles (trucks, rail cars) that will move raw materials to the plant and product to other plants of the company or customers are considered part of the new facility. This allows the materials handling system and all the related transportation network to be bought as an integrated system. The company estimates that it saves $500,000 annually from each major plant so designed and built.

UTILITIES

All industries require electric power of some sort. In most, power accounts for a small percentage of the total cost. But some, as aluminum reduction plants, require cheap energy in large amounts and as a result have historically located in the Northwest or some other place where hydroelectric power is available. Although nuclear power, magnetohydrodynamics, and other technological developments could alter the locational influence of power, it does not appear that this will occur before at least the 1990s.

Generally speaking, the typical public utility can supply power more cheaply than a company can generate its own. And while the cost of power will probably not be a determining factor in most site selections, the location decision maker should ask some pointed questions about the private utility and its capability to serve a new customer. Table 7 compares the energy costs of major cities in the fifty states and Puerto Rico.

An electrical utility should have a 50 to 20 percent reserve capacity, comments Fred P. Esbrandt of Baltimore Gas & Electric Company (BG&E).

During 1978, BG&E was one of the Eastern utilities still under a modified "new gas customer" moratorium. Esbrandt

TABLE 7 How Energy Consumption and Production, and Costs for Power, Coal, Oil and Gas Compare State by State

	Monthly bill 1978 1,000-kW demand; 400,000 kWh mo	Typical electrical power costs Demand ($/kW)	Typical electrical power costs Energy (¢/kWh)	Fuel power cost adjustment (¢/kWh)	Average cost, statewide industrial power (1977) (mils/kWh)
Alabama-Mobile	$11,620	$1.90	1.65	0.03	21.7
Alaska-Anchorage	9,444	1.70	1.00	—	32.4
Arizona-Phoenix	11,863	0.68–0.86	1.28	(7.37)	27.8
Arkansas-Fort Smith	10,188	1.15	0.44	1.41	23.4
California-Los Angeles	12,853	0.25	0.69	1.71	30.2
Colorado-Pueblo	11,652	1.36	1.79	0.41	20.3
Connecticut-Bridgeport	15,792	1.82	2.97	0.38	34.7
Delaware-Wilmington	14,785	1.83	1.90	1.14	32.0
Florida-Tampa	13,231	2.75	1.71	0.39	26.9
Georgia-Savannah	14,726	1.48	2.09	1.04	25.1
Hawaii-Honolulu	16,579	1.85	1.20	1.33	36.3
Idaho-Idaho Falls	4,584	1.68	0.72	—	12.0
Illinois-Chicago	13,092	2.78–3.26	1.14–1.93	0.32	24.7
Indiana-Indianapolis	9,795	4.22	1.17	0.20	24.6
Iowa-Waterloo	13,396	—	2.1	1.18	25.1
Kansas-Kansas City	12,103	1.45	0.66	1.23	25.0
Kentucky-Louisville	9,306	3.05+	0.78+	—	17.1
Louisiana-Baton Rouge	8,680	2.30	0.90	0.77	15.4
Maine-Portland	8,588	1.66	0.46	1.07	21.5
Maryland-Baltimore	12,176	2.16	1.00	—	27.4
Massachusetts-Springfield	13,209	3.25	0.30	0.94	40.6
Michigan-Detroit	13,487	4.97	1.57–1.77	0.54	29.3
Minnesota-St. Paul	13,037	4.64–5.62	1.57	0.01	27.9
Mississippi-Meridian	12,246	3.05+	0.78+	—	25.8
Missouri-St. Joseph	12,256	1.70	2.22	—	24.9
Montana-Billings	5,602	1.32	0.80	—	6.7
Nebraska-Omaha	7,319	1.40–3.80	1.10	(0.09)	19.2
Nevada-Reno	15,270	2.20	2.62	—	22.7
New Hampshire-Manchester	13,234	3.70	0.83	1.30	31.5
New Jersey-Jersey City	15,114	2.70	1.08	1.13	38.0
New Mexico-Albuquerque	15,126	3.10	0.75	0.64	
New York-Buffalo	11,075	3.11	1.16	0.85	28.6
North Carolina-Greensboro	10,575	—	1.38	0.15	23.1
North Dakota-Fargo	11,426	4.26	1.41	(0.01)	28.7
Ohio-Cincinnati	12,750	1.43	0.39	1.13	20.4
Oklahoma-Oklahoma City	9,914	1.21	0.75	1.06	21.4
Oregon-Portland	7,044	2.11	0.86	—	8.9
Pennsylvania-Pittsburgh	13,733	2.64	0.53	1.33	28.9
Puerto Rico-San Juan	21,460	—	—	—	—
Rhode Island-Providence	14,941	2.25	0.83	0.64	39.6
South Carolina-Charleston	11,824	4.06	0.97	0.69	21.6
SouthDakota-Rapid City	11,115	3.15	1.20	0.07	22.4
Tennessee-Memphis	8,928	3.05+	0.78+	—	18.2
Texas-Houston	9,019	3.25–5.60	0.91	0.41	21.5
Utah-Salt Lake City	9,356	3.32	1.20	—	21.7
Vermont-Burlington	11,134	1.65	1.70	0.40	26.0
Virginia-Norfolk	12,724	4.84	1.39	0.30	27.0
Washington-Seattle	3,005	0.45	0.35	—	4.3
West Virginia-Charleston	9,543	7.67	1.86	—	21.9
Wisconsin-Milwaukee	10,559	1.80–2.65	1.04	0.39	24.1
Wyoming-Cheyenne	4,446	2.54	0.68	—	13.1

+Rates in industrial power cost columns apply only to areas served by the Tennessee Valley Authority. ( ) credit. Notes: Demand and energy charges are low end of ranges which in the past have usually been the dominant components in total energy costs to large users. Fuel or power cost adjustment clauses, however, are now increasingly important in total energy costs. Value of such clauses are revised frequently. Figures under typical industrial power rate columns are only approximately comparable

Average fuel prices paid by steam-electric plants, statewide, March 1978 (¢/million Btu)			Average industrial natural gas prices, 1977 (¢/million Btu)	Crude oil reserves as of 12/31/77 (billions of bbl)	1976 (trillions of Btu)		Energy surplus or deficit	
Coal	Oil	Gas			Energy production	Energy consumption	as percent of personal income	in millions of dollars
135.8	281.9	214.9	137	0.044	786	1,488	-5.7%	$-1,074
—	—	—	076	9.62	570	239	10.8	421
39.1	238.8	116.0	125	—	313	698	-4.8	-632
81.1	190.5	111.2	114	0.086	301	697	-6.1	-648
—	251.3	220.6	200	3.63	2,580	5,059	-2.6	-3,959
63.8	175.0	131.0	111	0.242	642	831	-2.1	-351
—	211.4	—	298	—	136	755	-4.8	-1,102
135.7	209.3	154.1	203	—	none	185	-7.3	-309
161.1	193.1	96.1	119	0.209	400	1,977	5.3	2,686
110.5	223.9	220.5	138	—	88	1,408	-6.8	-1,870
—	—	—	658	—	none	191	-5.9	-355
—	—	—	193	—	115	302	-6.2	-296
147.8	257.3	410.8	186	0.150	1,693	3,910	-4.2	-3,526
158.3	268.8	165.4	149	0.026	587	2,251	-6.8	-2,267
107.8	261.1	168.4	134	—	46	937	-6.6	-1,216
91.1	191.2	116.3	119	0.360	1,261	942	1.6	243
140.3	287.3	104.3	143	0.035	3,611	1,275	8.6	1,595
—	183.7	98.7	137	3.11	11,245	2,770	48.6	10,059
—	—	—	302	—	79	324	-8.0	-459
127.9	198.3	—	218	—	154	1,185	-4.5	-1,590
—	189.2	177.0	271	—	44	1,112	6.5	2,181
141.8	272.1	194.3	186	0.133	422	2,815	-4.9	-3,122
74.5	206.6	151.5	146	—	110	1,235	-6.5	-1,581
147.4	190.2	152.6	146	0,203	345	623	-4.2	-457
148.1	241.6	105.2	133	—	134	1,506	-6.4	1,844
30.5	—	29.8	153	0.152	909	397	9.8	412
106.2	168.8	106.6	112	0.031	116	556	-6.3	-608
56.7	215.3	160.1	172	—	18	304	-8.0	-357
150.7	191.3	—	276	—	10	196	-6.5	-319
156.8	217.7	229.3	241	—	38	1,669	-5.0	-2,693
46.9	259.2	164.8	143	0.491	2,094	620	26.9	1,640
119.7	200.0	135.4	231	0.009	521	4,179	-4.7	-5,981
146.6	255.5	—	225	—	81	1,362	-6.0	-1,787
34.1	280.9	—	186	0.150	350	295	0.7	24
124.4	274.8	139.4	195	0.129	1,249	3,832	-5.0	-3,475
99.7	253.4	138.0	139	1.12	2,928	1,187	12.6	1,967
—	—	214.3	206	—	247	651	-4.5	-665
123.8	227.2	—	201	0.049	2,624	4,162	-3.8	-2,941
—	—	—	—	—	—	—	—	—
—	—	—	276	—	none	158	-4.6	-278
137.0	191.4	—	138	—	234	916	-6.6	-962
60.2	124.8	—	115	0.002	111	284	-7.6	-252
129.5	314.6	—	143	0.002	317	1,333	-6.2	-1,413
63.7	194.6	127.8	185	8.46	14,947	7,004	12.3	9,555
87.6	177.8	127.7	110	0.182	467	467	-1.0	-70
—	—	222.1	142	—	42	124	-5.8	-150
163.5	206.9	187.0	189	—	1,096	1,235	-3.1	-984
75.0	—	—	203	—	1,108	1,731	-4.2	-1,030
138.8	288.7	175.1	170	0.029	2,944	1,268	12.1	1,199
103.9	262.8	187.3	186	—	129	1,301	-5.5	-1,606
36.5	349.6	236.4	107	0.816	1,615	408	54.9	1,441

because of differences in utility rate schedules and because of various cost and tax adjustments, type of service, metering, certain discounts and load factors. Sources: Energy Information Administration, Edison Electric Institute, Chase Econometric Associates, Inc., American Gas Association.

SOURCE: *Chemical Week*, Nov. 1, 1978

suggests that companies using less than 20 percent gas in their process should turn their engineers loose to see if an alternative system can be devised. If it cannot, the company should check to see if its process fuel allotment is transferable. While the company might be able to transfer its allotment within the community, the likelihood is that it would be lost even with a move within the state.

Like most utility people, Esbrandt maintains a file of available industrial real estate, knows the important public and private contacts who can answer your questions, and can provide additional insights into the possible compatibility of a company and community.

Reliability has probably become the most important factor from an energy standpoint. For that reason, some companies have elected to build their own power sources. But most companies still look to purchase their needs from a public or private utility.

Many industries view site selection and building construction as a means to cut energy costs.[3] Out of energy cost awareness more industrial plants are being built partially underground to take advantage of the constant temperatures found there plus the insulating effect of bermed earth.

The return to coal could increase the attractiveness of West Virginia and western Pennsylvania and of such western states as Wyoming, Montana, and South Dakota. Also, the oil- and gas-rich Gulf States continue to attract energy-dependent industries, while other areas such as the Pacific Northwest and New Jersey, the eastern regions of Maryland and Delaware, and Long Island hope that the promise of oil and gas in the Atlantic will provide a new base for industrial growth.

The concept of an "energy park," where several companies share a utility, has also received renewed attention, although no trend appears to be developing. Heavy manufacturing firms, of course, use the most power and often prefer to build their own utility. Complicating the decision today are supply-cost questions related to fuel oil, coal, and nuclear sources and to the timetable for comparably priced solar energy. We believe that the uncertainties will remain through the 1980s and that energy parks will continue to be more a gimmick for use by developers and municipalities than a viable idea that should be a prime factor for companies in weighing one location against another.

Most utilities such as BG&E point to nuclear power as the energy source of the future. BG&E already has 60 percent of its needs supplied by nuclear energy and new capacity under construction will boost that percentage. While electric utility companies are not aggressively pursuing new business, most have the capacity to accommodate it. On the other hand, less than half of the gas utilities (mostly those east of the Mississippi River) could accept a new customer and only about one-third could add a new customer without some restrictions—such as a clause for interruptible service.

ENVIRONMENTAL FACTORS

Steel and aluminum production, synthetic rubber manufacture, and a number of chemical processes require large quantities of process water. While public supplies will often suffice, hard water can prove damaging to equipment and may be one reason why few other industries have chosen the location that looks so favorable at first consideration. Surface waters from lakes and streams can vary considerably in chemical content and at some stage the location decision maker should verify the quantity and quality of the water supply.

In these days of increasing environmental concerns, waste disposal continues to gain in importance as a cost item for industrial plants. Again, though most public utilities can handle the normal sanitary sewage disposal requirements of a company, the treatment of process water may have to be handled separately. And don't assume that just because you return the water the way that you get it that you will be in compliance. Strange as it may seem, companies have been forced to treat even their cooling water because the influent water (also the local drinking water) did not meet federal EPA regulations for effluent.

In general, state pollution control programs may affect the location of industrial activity in two ways. First, the effect on production costs from air and water quality standards varies by state because the level, comprehensiveness, and enforcement of such standards is not uniform among states.[4] Second, many states facilitate industrial compliance of state air and water quality standards by providing public waste treatment facilities, tax exemptions for pollution abatement facilities, and/or tax-exempt status for bonds to finance pollution abatement facilities. Since this type of assistance reduces production costs and varies among states, the location of industrial activity may shift toward states providing greater economic incentives for pollution control. It appears that the way states attempt to gain industrial compliance of pollution control could become an important industrial site selection factor, especially for the major polluting industries.

Finally, companies should not ignore the benefits that can come from a geographical clustering. Direct-cost benefits evolve from the increased demand for interchangeable factors of production and transportation that result when a number of plants locate within a single industrial complex.

Indirect-cost reductions stem from other benefits realized from location in close proximity to an industrial population.

Examples of direct-cost reductions are (1) lower total transfer costs resulting from better transport facilities, (2) reduced production costs due to a ready supply of technically trained labor, and (3) specialization of supplies, allowing lower unit costs for materials, supplies, and services.

Indirect costs are not as easily quantified. A particular type of insurance may be available because of better protective facilities· or familiarity of an insurance company with local hazards.

CLIMATE CONSIDERATIONS

With energy costs now accounting for a larger portion of the operating costs of a facility, some considerations of climate may be appropriate. Based on national energy consumption data, heating takes the largest share followed in order by lighting, cooling, power for equipment, and domestic hot water.[5] Figure 10 summarizes data produced by Dubin-Bloome Associates and the National Bureau of Standards using computer analysis. The drawing illustrates the relative energy consumption for an identical office building if located in Manchester, New Hampshire, or Orlando, Florida. As shown, the order of magnitude for the five variables will differ with climate. Of course, the function of the building and its design, construction, and operation also make a difference.

In climatic zones with mild winters of below 2500 degree-days (see Figure 11), the seasonal cooling load may be larger than the seasonal heating load, as shown in Figure 10 for Orlando. In the mild zone, the cost for lighting may exceed

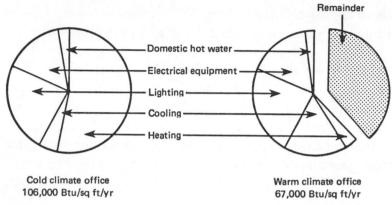

Cold climate office
106,000 Btu/sq ft/yr

Warm climate office
67,000 Btu/sq ft/yr

FIG. 10   The difference in energy requirements for operating office buildings in warm and cold climates. (SOURCE: Fred S. Dubin and Chalmers G. Long, Jr., *Energy Conservation Standards*, McGraw-Hill, New York, 1978, p. 5.)

that for either heating or cooling. In cold climates (6000 degree-days annually and above), heating in office buildings usually consumes the most energy per year, with lighting and cooling next. In mid-range climates (2500 to 6000 degree-days annually), the ordering of categories depends largely upon the type of mechanical and electrical systems and the characteristics of the building structure in which they are installed.

The location on the site and the layout and quality of construction can all increase or decrease the energy efficiency of a particular facility. While these factors require evaluation by a competent engineer and are outside the limits of this book, locational decision makers should keep energy costs and future availability of energy in mind when weighing one geographical area against another and when choosing the final site and purchasing, leasing, or constructing a facility.

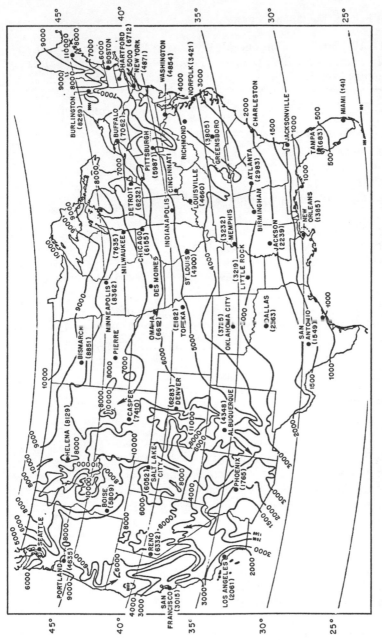

FIG. 11 Annual mean heating degree-days below 65°F. A heating degree-day is an average temperature 1° below a given temperature base (in this case 65°F). A day with an average temperature of 60°F thus has 5 degree-days. The map gives the degree-day totals for all days of the year with average temperatures below the base 65°F. (SOURCE: *Climatic Atlas of the United States*, Department of Commerce, June 1968, p. 70.)

FIG. 12 Site selection checklist. (SOURCE: *Factory Management and Maintenance*, May 1957, pp. 180+. Reprinted by permission of Morgan-Gampian Company.)

	Importance	*Site*
12. Electric Power		
Can power system fill your needs (voltage, phase, cycles, capacity)?	☐	☐
If relocating equipment do motor characteristics coincide with supply?	☐	☐
Can distribution lines handle a plant expansion program?	☐	☐
Is history of stoppages favorable?	☐	☐
Is complete rate picture satisfactory?	☐	☐
Are off-peak rates available?	☐	☐
Do discounts and penalties apply?	☐	☐
Are lighting allowances figured into rates?	☐	☐
Are fuel adjustment clauses provided for in rate schedules of power companies?	☐	☐
Are you planning to manufacture part or all of your own electric power?	☐	☐
Will nuclear power be available?		
13. Fuel Oil		
Is oil a competitive fuel in the area?	☐	☐
Can you count on delivery regardless of method (pipe-line, tank car, tank truck, barge, tanker)?	☐	☐
Do all component factors look favorable? (Tappable trunk line nearby, pipeline capacity, pumping capacity, rate picture, BTU content, proximity to gas fields, etc.?)	☐	☐
14. Natural Gas	☐	☐
Is natural gas a competitive fuel in area?	☐	☐
Is gas available on a firm basis?	☐	☐
Are rates such that it is better to arrange for interruptible basis with standby fuel oil facilities?	☐	☐

15. Coal	*Importance*	*Site*
Is coal a competitive fuel in the area?	☐	☐
Any problems about delivery?	☐	☐
Have you considered costs of coal handling and storage facilities vs. competitive fuels?	☐	☐
Do technological improvements in mining and usage help tilt the balance toward coal?	☐	☐
Should lignite be considered?	☐	☐

16. Water Supply

	Importance	*Site*
Are water requirements compatible with water resources?	☐	☐
Is there an adequate public water supply?	☐	☐
If you must exploit a private source, is the quantity adequate?	☐	☐
Is quality satisfactory?	☐	☐
If water treatment is needed, are costs in line with other site locations?	☐	☐
If streams are the logical source, will the flow be adequate during dry months?	☐	☐
Is the impact of future municipal and industrial users likely to be serious?	☐	☐
If ground water is the source, are there legal restrictions on withdrawal and recharging rates of flow?	☐	☐
Is there enough water to take care of growing trends toward air conditioning?	☐	☐
Is incoming temperature of cooling water satisfactory?	☐	☐
Are municipal authorities taking a long forward look at community water problems?	☐	☐
Do technological improvements offer help in the water problem?	☐	☐

FIG. 12 (*Continued*)

---

17. Water Pollution	*Importance*	*Site*
Will you have waste disposal problems?	☐	☐
Can streams nearby accommodate waste water?	☐	☐
Will good business practice plus local or state ordinances call for waste treatment?		

18. Raw Material Supply

Are needed raw materials close enough? (Especially if perishables, bulky, or low in value).	☐	☐
Will they be available, or are they committed to others?	☐	☐
Are raw material sources reliable?	☐	☐
Are the prices satisfactory?	☐	☐
Are terms of sale and delivery right?	☐	☐
Is cost of transport to site reasonable?	☐	☐
Do you see evidence of depletion or shortage of resources (minerals, timber, soil, water, others)?	☐	☐
Are there natural transportation transfer points nearby?	☐	☐
Are suppliers of key parts or subassemblies close enough?	☐	☐
Is rapid transportation from suppliers by truck or other means available?	☐	☐
Are you close enough to key suppliers for easy consultation?	☐	☐
Are existing or proposed manufacturers nearby whose byproducts you can use?	☐	☐
Are raw materials so remote that you must consider building homes and facilities for workers to attract them?	☐	☐
Where large natural resource areas are needed (such as timber or ores) can they be leased or must they be bought?	☐	☐
Have you attempted to forecast new sources?	☐	☐

	Importance	Site
Are multiple supply areas available in case of short supply from one?	☐	☐

19. Physical Climate

Has your general location survey thoroughly
explored climatic conditions? Typical factors: ☐   ☐
a. General weather conditions.
b. Elevation of community.
c. Temperature ranges and averages.
d. Average annual rainfall and snowfall.
e. Humidity ranges and averages.
f. Days with sunshine, rain, fog.
g. Duration of killing frost.
h. Low subsistence rates of South: clothing,
   heating, farming.
i. Low maintenance costs of South—no frost
   (building and road maintenance) snow and
   ice removal.
j. Velocity and direction of prevailing winds.
k. Geographical extremes? For example:
   unusual or prolonged dry or wet
   conditions; cold, heat, hurricanes, floods,
   etc.
l. Degree days per season.
m. Effect of weather extremes on all forms of
   transportation? Rail, highway, air, water.

NOTES

1. Donald J. Bowersox, *Logistical Management*, Macmillan, New York, 1974, p. 484.
2. "Transportation—The Key Element In Geo-Economic Planning," reproduced from *Site Selection Handbook*, February

1976, pp. 77–82, by permission of the publisher, Conway Publications, Inc., Atlanta, Georgia. No further reproduction is permitted.

3. "Change Your Checklist," reproduced from *Site Selection Handbook*, September 1977, pp. 250–256, by permission of the publisher, Conway Publications, Inc., Atlanta, Georgia. No further reproduction is permitted.

4. Keith R. Leitner, *Effect of State Pollution Control Programs on Industrial Location*, Ph.D. dissertation, Kansas State University, 1974.

5. Fred S. Dubin and Chalmers G. Long, *Energy Conservation Standards*, McGraw-Hill, New York, 1978, pp. 2–5.

SEVEN

Hand-Picking
Your Community

Should you locate your facility in or near a large metropolitan city, a smaller city, or a rural area? Each has its attraction as a place to live. The sheer size and variety of a metropolis make it a very special place. And major urban areas usually have the specialized labor force and transportation networks many companies need. On the other hand, the rural community usually provides a cleaner, safer environment for workers.

Our purpose in this chapter is not to suggest a choice. Rather, we will outline some of the attractions provided by different types of communities and point out past and present trends that might influence their future character.

For a potential location to be considered a "community," it must be a place where (1) local values can be set and enforced, (2) local residents can make a living, (3) close personal relationships can be developed, and (4) by collective action the people can accomplish tasks too large—or too urgent—to be handled by a single person.[1]

Sociologists call folk-village intimacy *Gemeinschaft* and

urban impersonality *Gesellschaft*. Gemeinschaft is the feeling of community that stems from a similarity of viewpoints and life-styles. It is a sense of belonging that arises from family relationships, friendships, and shared religious activities. Gesellschaft applies to the urban associations that depend more on logic and rationality—relationships that are specialized and defined by rules.

Perhaps the most enduring of the theories of city structure was created by sociologists at the University of Chicago in the 1920s. It suggests that urban communities grow outward in zones from a primary core in the central business district. The second zone, called a zone of transition because it lies in the path of business expansion, is populated mainly by low-income residents, migrants, and social outcasts. The third zone consists of workingmen's homes; the fourth is a zone of middle-class inhabitants, mostly professionals; while the fifth, the outer ring of the city, is populated by well-to-do commuters.

Subdivision into residential areas helps create what sociologist Lewis Wirth called the mosaic of social worlds that constitutes the city. Wirth characterized the urban community as having distinctive attributes, different from those of smaller aggregations of people. Because a metropolis is large, dense, and culturally varied, it has an impersonal mode of life he called *urbanism*. Places of work and recreation are generally situated away from the district where the individual lives, bringing contact with many different people. Because human activities are so specialized in the city, the urban dweller is often extremely dependent on these people *en masse*, but less dependent on them individually than would be the case in a small town. It is *urbanism*, as Wirth defines it, that gives rise to so many of the features of city life that bewilder and antagonize newcomers and prompt them to characterize the studied withdrawal—an essential mechanism of self-defense—as rudeness.

THE BIG CITY

The County and City Data Book 1977 lists 25 urbanized areas that have a population of more than one million, according to the 1970 U.S. Census (Table 8). This list also shows 123 urban areas with populations of 100,000 to one million, and 98 with a population between 50,000 and 100,000.

As has been suggested in earlier chapters, the movement of corporations out of the center city to the suburbs gained momentum in the 1960s and continues today, with moves from the North and Midwest to the South the latest trend. Why?

The New York City question has been studied in depth by Wolfgang Quante.[2] Between 1968 and 1974, forty of New York City's Fortune-500 companies chose to move their corporate headquarters. Among them were General Electric, Shell Oil, and American Can. About 70 percent of the New York City exits were to New York, New Jersey, and Connecticut areas within the metropolitan region.

Not only do such relocations remove the companies from the city's tax rolls, but they take workers away and make it more difficult for retail shops, restaurants, and other types of business and professional services (particularly small firms) to survive. Moreover, as other companies see the success of such moves, it prompts them to consider the same step.

TABLE 8 Population of the Top Twenty-five Urbanized Areas in Rank Order

Rank	Area	1970 Population
1	New York, N.Y.–Northeastern, N.J.	16,206,841
2	Los Angeles–Long Beach, Calif.	8,351,266
3	Chicago, Ill.–Northwestern, Ind.	6,714,578
4	Philadelphia, Pa.–N.J.	4,021,042
5	Detroit, Mich.	3,970,584
6	San Francisco–Oakland, Calif.	2,987,850
7	Boston, Mass.	2,652,575
8	Washington, D.C.–Md.-Va.	2,481,459
9	Cleveland, Ohio	1,959,880
10	St. Louis, Mo.–Ill.	1,882,944
11	Pittsburgh, Pa.	1,846,042
12	Minneapolis–St. Paul, Minn.	1,700,725
13	Houston, Tex.	1,677,863
14	Baltimore, Md.	1,579,582
15	Dallas, Tex.	1,338,684
16	Milwaukee, Wis.	1,252,457
17	Seattle–Everett, Wash.	1,238,107
18	Miami, Fla.	1,219,661
19	San Diego, Calif.	1,198,323
20	Altanta, Ga.	1,172,778
21	Cincinnati, Ohio–Ky.	1,110,514
22	Kansas City, Mo.–Kans.	1,101,949
23	Buffalo, N.Y.	1,086,594
24	Denver, Colo.	1,047,311
25	San Jose, Calif.	1,025,273

SOURCE: *County and City Data Book 1977*, U.S. Department of Commerce, Bureau of the Census, 1978, p. 802.

There are three basic reasons for the relocations:

1. *Pull factors.* Response to the demographic redistributions of present and potential employees who are considered necessary to the successful operation of a company.
2. *Push factors.* The city's high corporate and personal

income taxes, lack of sufficient numbers of clerical workers, the unavailability of suitable housing, problems in the public schools, and the high incidence of crime. All these add up to a higher cost of doing business in New York City.

3. *Technology factors.* Advancements in telecommunications, transportation, electronics, data processing, and other means of information collection and communication have made it possible to locate a corporate headquarters nearly anywhere within the United States (although the Eastern time zone and access to the financial world of New York City and the seat of government in Washington, D.C., still seem to be important considerations).

For New York City, a part of its attraction has been its image of superiority as both the country's management and social center. Maintenance of that image will affect the City's future.

A study of the relocation of Los Angeles' firms finds that as manufacturing plants expand, the predominant trend is outward from the central core area.[3] Distinct labor skill categories affect the distance and direction of movement. Also, firms exploiting economics of large scale move greater distances from the core area. The movements occur along declining wage rate and land rent gradients radiating from the core.

Research into the industrial makeup of the Baltimore region reveals additional insights into city-suburb characteristics. Among the major findings:[4]

1. Baltimore's industrial establishments were primarily oriented to intraregional markets, whereas outlying establishments were mainly oriented to out-of-region markets.

2. On a comparative basis, nearly three times as many industrial establishments in Baltimore were located in multiple occupancy buildings as in the outlying zone.

3. Industrial establishments in Baltimore City were found to use proportionately more building space for warehousing than their suburban counterparts.

4. Real estate taxes and building rentals for Baltimore-based industrial establishments, viewed from the standpoint of square feet of building area, were less than for outlying areas in corresponding Standard Industrial Code (SIC) Groups.

5. Industrial establishments in Baltimore had an insignificantly lower proportion of unskilled employees than the outlying establishments.

6. Throughout the region, the highest proportion of unskilled employees worked in warehousing, skilled workers were engaged in the manufacturing activity, and professional workers were employed in nonmanufacturing.

Peter A. Morrison, a senior staff member of the Rand Corporation's social science department, studied the dissimilar effects of common demographic processes on a city enjoying rapid population growth (San José, California) and one suffering from central-city population decline (St. Louis).

Impacting on both cities, he suggests, have been changes in the migratory patterns of the United States population. With net immigration down to only 0.2 percent of the United States population from the 0.6 percent in the early part of the century, and the rate of rural-to-urban migration slowing, major cities have had to depend on other factors for growth. In the case of San José, it has benefited from a migration flow from other urban areas—namely, San Francisco and Los Angeles. Moreover, many of San José's residents are young prospective parents, and the city has relatively few elderly persons. These factors, suggests Morrison, lay a broad foundation for the population's continued growth through natural increase, despite the national downturn in fertility. During the 1965–1970 period, San José had a net migration gain of 35,373. But with about 21 migrants entering and 17 departing each year per 100 residents, the growth rests on a precarious arithmetic balance.

"The outward dispersal of population from central cities that has occurred in St. Louis has been accelerating in other cities as well, and will remain a prominent feature of U.S. urban growth." points out Morrison. Since 1965, the white population has ceased to replace itself, its death rate having exceeded its birth rate. On the other hand, the city's black population has not undergone severe migratory change and has retained its strong replacement capacity (Table 9). However, beginning in 1969 the black population also began to decline, perhaps indicating that the number of entering migrants has begun decreasing.

According to Morrison:

> In cities like St. Louis, where population is dispersing but old political boundaries are fixed, the problems of the central city are separated from the resources in the suburbs. Transitional problems associated with persistent and severe out-migration also arise: accumulation of advantaged citizens, declining demand for city housing and a diminished replacement capacity in the population. Carried far enough, the last of these problems results in natural decrease, and thereafter the population's decline acquires its own dynamics. As noted earlier, the white population in St. Louis has reached this

TABLE 9 Components of Population Change in
St. Louis, 1960 to 1970

Data are expressed as rates of change per 100 residents in
1960.

	Total change	Natural increase*	Net migration
	Both races		
St. Louis SMSA	12.3	11.5	0.8
St. Louis city	−17.0	7.3	−24.4
Remainder of SMSA†	28.5	13.8	14.7
	Whites		
St. Louis SMSA	9.4	10.1	−0.7
St. Louis city	−31.6	2.4	−34.0
Remainder of SMSA†	26.6	13.3	13.3
	Nonwhites		
St. Louis SMSA	28.2	20.2	9.7
St. Louis city	18.6	19.5	−0.4
Remainder of SMSA†	53.8	22.0	37.2

*Rate of increase attributed to excess births over deaths.
†Metropolitan ring.

‡In this section of the table, "total change" applies only
to the black population. "Natural increase" and "net migration" apply to the nonwhite population as a whole, but virtually all nonwhites in the St. Louis SMSA are blacks.

SOURCE: Peter A. Morrison, "Urban Growth and Decline:
San Jose and St. Louis in the 1960's," *Science*, Volume 185,
p. 759, copyright August 30, 1974, by The American Association for the Advancement of Science.

point: The number of persons dying now exceeds the number being born.[5]

Moreover, notes Morrison, the black migration out of the
city is now more than enough to cancel the growth through
natural increase.

WRITE OFF THE METROPOLIS?

Does this mean that the major cities are either dead or dying and that companies should avoid them? Not necessarily. The major urban centers still represent a reservoir of skilled and unskilled labor and with high unemployment offer a readily available work force. What's more, many cities now appear to be stabilizing and have begun fighting back with programs designed to encourage existing industry to stay and others to return or make an initial investment.

A 1972 doctoral thesis by William C. Wheaton, *Income and Urban Location*, suggests that the tide could begin to flow back to the city. Using income data on consumption and location from San Francisco, Wheaton evaluated seven groups of families representing differences in income, family size, and age levels. Two conclusions were drawn: First, the influence of greater income per se always leads to more peripheral locations. Conversely, the difference in taste that accompanies rising income implies more central locations. But, finds the study, *the influence of taste dominates that of additional spending power.*

"The fact that the location outcome of this 'instantaneous city' is just the opposite of the present pattern in San Francisco," noted Wheaton, "suggests that the existing arrangement must have resulted from the historical influence of low income immigration and deteriorating housing."[6]

Indeed, what social scientists now see taking place in San Francisco is "urban gentrification," the return of the middle class—usually white, professional couples—to older neighborhoods. And what's happening in San Francisco's Haight-Ashbury is taking place around the country, e.g., in the Old Town section of Alexandria, Virginia, and the Society Hill section of Philadelphia.

95

Although business deserted the Haight in the 1960s, observes Marilyn Chase in *The Wall Street Journal*, "today an economic revival is under way, drawing new kinds of business and residents. The head shops and crash pads of the psychedelic past are giving way to professional offices and boutiques, chic bars and beautifully restored Victorian houses." Commercial vacancy now registers 10 percent as compared with 40 percent in 1970.[7]

The U.S. Department of Housing and Urban Development cites Baltimore as the best example of revitalization of downtown residential areas. Baltimore won an "All American City" designation in 1976 for its overall redevelopment program. Included was the revitalizing of the Inner Harbor, where new high-rise office buildings, a new convention center, an aquarium, the World Trade Center building of the Baltimore Port Authority, the Maryland Science Center, and Harbor Place have been built or begun.

All of these projects have been accomplished through a strong cooperation between government and industry. For example, when completed, Harbor Place will be a $15-million complex of restaurants and shops. However, these are being built while the ethnic flavor of traditional Baltimore is being strengthened and maintained. One means of accomplishing the latter has been through city-sponsored folk festivals in the Inner Harbor area.

The movement of companies from the Northeast and West to the Sunbelt may not be the easy escape from the social and economic problems of the urban Midwest and East that it first appears. Gurney Breckenfeld, in a 1977 *Fortune* article, "Business Loves the Sunbelt (and Vice Versa)," observes that "the black population, 16 percent of the Sunbelt, has scarcely shared in the economic upsurge." Rather, companies have located where they can find underemployed white labor partly because their education level tends to be somewhat higher and they are not as likely to join a union as are blacks. Breckenfeld adds that

> As a result, many black rural poor are moving to southern big cities where they are forming large racial and economic ghettos. The trend is a time bomb that could explode and upset the region's present tranquility. . . . In cities, the gulf between the rich and poor becomes more tangible, more likely to stir wrath or even riot. . . . Few Sunbelt political or business leaders seem to have paid enough attention to such problems as yet, though the evidence is piling up that big Sunbelt cities are committing some of the mistakes that have led northern cities into trouble, plus a few of their own.[8]

Thus, while the cost advantages provided by Sunbelt cities will probably continue for some time, Atlanta, New Orleans, Houston, Dallas, Charlotte, and a few other cities already show compartmentalized growth patterns with clusters of well-to-do whites, poor whites, poor blacks and in some cases poor Mexican-Americans. The focus, suggests Breckenfeld, is apt to switch to smaller metropolitan areas and towns in the countryside, paralleling the trend already underway elsewhere in the United States.

THE SUBURBS

Cities have long fought their suburbs. One way a city can combat uncontrolled growth around its edges is by annexation. This provides control over the zoning of the land around the urban core and allows orderly and controlled growth with construction of adequate municipal services such as sewers and schools. Properly conducted, annexation includes the poor as well as the rich suburbs, takes place before an area is extensively developed, fits into a master plan for the city and its environs, and commits the city to take on the leadership and responsibility of tackling the problems of the fringe community.

Other options open to a city include limited annexation, where the city gains control over the development of an area and in turn supplies sanitation and other city services. Another method is the creation of a special purpose district—a compromise whereby an area that has resisted city control allows that control in exchange for restricted zoning (e.g., one-acre minimum lots or houses within a certain price range). Also, sometimes the county government can and will exercise control if prompted by the municipality.

What it all adds up to is the fact that the problem of a community cannot be solved well by drawing up separate plans for housing, traffic, parks and recreation, schools and industry, and shopping. Proper decentralization of the cities means developing self-sustaining communities, not creating parasite communities. A collection of suburbs does not make a satisfactory city.

Because of the rapid expansion of suburban communities, their inhabitants are all strangers in the beginning. The roots that grow in villages and city neighborhoods from childhood friendships and lifelong residence are generally lacking. Even crucial family ties may be stretched by distance. In the United States during the 1970s, nearly one-fifth of the population moved every year. This isolation is accelerated by the commuter's work pattern. Absent at a distant job from early morning until late evening, the worker must expend considerable effort to establish relationships with fellow community members—indeed, to maintain close relationships with one's own spouse and children is difficult. Yet in most suburbs, the residents get to know one another fairly well, and a sense of community does arise.

One problem of a suburb tends to be homogeneity—most of the inhabitants tend to be around the same age and same income level and thus some of the adventure and vitality of the city are lost. In exchange, the suburban dweller obtains some elbow room and a personal haven away from the social problems and congestion of the city.

Companies move for many of the same reasons. The land costs within the city have risen so high that multistory buildings are a necessity. Often, the real estate taxes have climbed substantially as cities seek to recoup revenues lost from the leaving of other companies and from the exit of the upper and middle class. And workers begin to worry about their safety coming to and from the job. Seldom have urban companies had the foresight to provide adequate off-street parking for their employees.

But as the suburbs grow so, too, grow the problems. Not only are road systems frequently inadequate and overloaded but likewise the sewage-disposal systems. Public transportation systems tend to be infrequent or nonexistent, creating a totally automobile dependent society. And local residents often fight the prospects of an industrial plant that could help ease the tax revenue bind.

SMALL CITIES AND TOWNS

What, then, of the smaller cities and towns?

Not too surprisingly, it is those nonmetropolitan areas that have ample supplies of adequate quality labor, a favorable business climate, and a favorable physical climate that tend to attract manufacturing industry.[9]

A recent study found that the major locational factors

that attract companies to communities of 2500 to 50,000 population were primarily economic and not those considerations, such as property taxes, which are controlled by public decision makers. Moreover, the amenity variables were observed to correlate closely with the economic variables (distance to metropolitan area, labor force, personal services, transportation services, and closeness to suppliers and markets).[10]

While not limited to just small towns, a survey of manufacturing plants in Mississippi that employ twenty-five or more persons examined the "Important Influence and Adequacy Factors" that prompted the decision to locate the plant in Mississippi. The top five factors were attitudes of local officials, attitudes of local citizens, availability of desired land, favorable wage scale, and labor attitudes.[11]

What this all adds up to is that locational decision makers tend to look for the same basic factors in the nonmetropolitan areas as urban regions. The added consideration appears to be more attention to the attitudes of local community leaders and local labor toward a new employer. One good reason for this is that the zoning covenants and other protections which are provided almost automatically by the urbanized areas may have to be aggressively sought and won from a small community.

One-industry towns, in particular, may have an antigrowth bias.[12] Such towns arise because certain types of firms perceive a locational advantage in a small community—an advantage that will persist only if they are successful in repulsing other industries. The dominant type of industry in southern towns will most likely be low-wage, labor-intensive firms such as textile mills and apparel plants. In nonsouthern towns, a wide diversity of industrial types are commonly found.

NEW CITIES

"It has required an unprecedented series of shocks—burning rivers, municipal strikes, student violence—to rouse a complacent America to the urgency of remaking its centers of urban culture into fit places for people," observes Gurney Breckenfeld. He adds:

> The problems have been around for decades, steadily worsening. . . . Irreversible decay seemed to grip big U.S. cities as they struggled ineffectually with crime, drugs, congestion, racial tension, bad schools, and worse housing. . . . In hope of escaping such troubles, middle-class families for years have been spreading out into the suburbs, to the point that mile upon mile of once sylvan enclaves have become 'slurbs'—half-city and half-country places combining the worst features of both. [13]

One attempt to provide orderly growth has been the planned city. Such cities trace their modern history to Ebenezer Howard who sought to build garden cities on the outskirts of London in the early 1900s. Revived after World War II by Britain's The New Towns Act of 1946, a number of new towns on the London periphery again sprung up, each aimed at populations of 50,000 to 60,000. Perhaps to be expected, these towns have attracted middle-income workers and have low unemployment. As a corollary, the concentration of older, unskilled workers in the major cities has increased.

Like the thirty or so new towns in Britain since the mid-1940s, about thirty other new towns have been built in Western Europe to reduce the pressure of population of major cities. Most were for social purposes rather than as profit-making ventures. For example, in Sweden the new towns are at the extremities of Stockholm's municipal subway system. Stockholm planners promoted suburban expansion and by the year 2000 hope that the population of the city's inner core will only be 17 percent as compared with about 27 percent in 1970.

The concept of the garden city in the United States traces its recent history to Clarence P. Stein, a New York City architect. His first venture was Sunnyside Gardens, Queens, which provided low-cost housing for families of moderate means. Franklin Roosevelt's New Deal brought Stein the opportunity to build three new towns—Greenbelt, Maryland, Greenhills, Ohio, and Greendale, Wisconsin. After Roosevelt, the greenbelt towns passed through a number of unsympathetic bureaucratic hands and by 1949 all except Greendale, Wisconsin, had been carved up and sold to private developers.

By the early 1950s a number of private developers began to build large look-alike communities such as Levittown, Pennsylvania, and Levittown, Long Island, both the brainchildren of William J. Levitt. In the 1960s, a number of large corporations such as Chrysler and U.S. Steel jumped into the land business. Most of these efforts were financed by selling stock to the public and differed little from conventional subdivisions. Others were vacation home developments or retirement cities. Nearly all lacked primary employment and fell short of providing cultural, recreational, and educational facilities and thus were not "genuine" new towns.

Several corporations took advantage of federal guaranteed loans beginning in the late 1960s, and such cities as Gananda (New York), Jonathan (Minnesota), and Flower Mound (Texas) were born. By late 1978, these, too, had been broken up and sold to private developers after millions of dollars of public funds had been spent for roadways, sewage systems, and other public services.

On the other hand, there have been some notable successes, particularly Columbia (Maryland), Reston (Virginia), and Irvine (California).

The land for Columbia, Maryland, at its time of purchase in the mid-1960s, was predominately rural. It is being developed by the Howard Research and Development Corporation, a joint venture of The Rouse Company and Connecticut General Insurance Corporation. Located about midway between Baltimore and Washington, D.C., the 22 square miles (about 15,000 acres) constitutes nearly 10 percent of Howard County. "What makes Columbia unique," notes Breckenfeld, "is neither its layout (which is sensitive but largely unoriginal) nor its architecture (which is conservatively contemporary though seldom stodgy). Columbia's innovations—and its exemplary triumphs—lie in urban sociology."[14]

To produce the best possible environment for the growth of people, The Rouse Company convened a group of fourteen sociologists, ministers, and other "people experts" regularly over a period of several months during the city's planning stage. Other objectives were: to provide a complete and self-sustaining city with an eventual population of 100,000 in order to support the commercial and cultural activities that make a city complete; to respect the land by providing parks, playgrounds, artificial lakes, and recreational facilities such as golf courses; and to make a profit. "Only by being a financial success," James W. Rouse, chairman of The Rouse Company, told us, "can Columbia become a model for other cities that do more than add to an existing urban sprawl."

As Breckenfeld observed, Columbia has been more than

just an opportunistic venture: The shape of Columbia, eight villages clustered around a downtown urban core, "arose partly from the nature of the site and partly from its creator's convictions. . . . Columbia's physical plan evolved into three interlocking entities: neighborhoods with 900 to 1,200 families, villages with 3,000 to 5,000 families, and the town as a whole."[15]

Over one-third of the total land area of Columbia is permanently reserved for recreation and open space. A unique quasi-public organization, The Columbia Association, maintains the open space and provides most of the recreational amenities such as swimming pools, playgrounds, and pathways.

Each neighborhood has an elementary school and each village a middle school (junior high); several villages also have a senior high school. There are three colleges, and downtown adjacent to a large shopping mall are theaters, mid-rise apartments, and other public services and office buildings. A unique feature of Columbia is its health and medical arrangements. Baltimore's Johns Hopkins Medical Institutions, in conjunction with Connecticut General Insurance Corporation, set up a prepaid, group practice health care plan that for a fixed monthly fee entitles participants to almost total medical care, including surgery and hospitalization. The Columbia Medical Plan, as it is now known, has more than 100 full- and part-time physicians and medical technologists on its staff.

Now, just slightly more than twelve years after the first spade was turned in 1967, Columbia has a population of about 55,000 and has developed twelve business parks in which over 26,000 people work.

What has James Rouse been most pleased with? "The realization that Columbia today is as close to our expectations and hopes as it is. We believe this is because the design stage of the city tried to get at the root of what works for people and what makes life good. The village life concept has worked. Each community has its own special flavor, active citizenry and feeling of creativity—that they can, and will, have an impact on the nature of village life."

THE RURAL OPTION

Rural areas are considerably more limited than urbanized areas in their ability to provide for the needs of industry. A study was made of the counties of Illinois, Georgia, and Ohio in which the largest city contained fewer than 25,000 people; in 1970 there were 81 such counties in Illinois, 145 in Georgia, and 63 in Ohio.[16] Table 10 summarizes the general findings.

TABLE 10 Dimensions of Socioeconomic Structure in Nonmetropolitan Illinois, Georgia, and Ohio

Factors*	Illinois	Georgia	Ohio
Factor I	Urban orientation	Urban orientation	Urban orientation
Factor II	Agricultural prosperity	Labor availability	Agricultural prosperity
Factor III	Regional market Proximity/urban agglomeration economies	Agricultural prosperity	Labor availability
Factor IV	Manufacturing growth	Regional market proximity	Manufacturing growth
Factor V	Activity in mineral industries	Population age	Local infrastructure
Factor VI	—	Manufacturing growth	Local business activity

*Ranked according to their degree of importance.
SOURCE: Ronald J. Swager, "Locational Requirements of Selected Industries in Nonmetropolitan Areas," *AIDC Journal*, vol. XII, October 1977, p. 16.

As shown, urban orientation appears to be the single most important dimension. (*Urban orientation* refers to a county's "degree of urban-ness" rather than its physical proximity to a metropolitan area and is derived from population-type variables.) Agricultural growth and manufacturing growth are additional factors of importance.

The other major conclusion that can be drawn from Table 10 is that rural areas differ considerably in character and as a result any attempts to explain industrial location factors must be restricted to a regional scale. Table 11 expands this data for thirty-two industries in Georgia. Listings are by three-digit SIC (Standard Industrial Classification) codes, and the statistical measures illustrate the degree of importance of each factor for each industry; values are not comparable between industries. A minus sign means simply that a factor is usually absent and thus not required for the particular industry (it does not mean that the presence of the factor would inhibit an industry.)

As can be seen, labor availability is more than twice as important as any other factor to the most rapidly expanding industry in rural Georgia, the floor covering mills industry (SIC 227). The secondary requirements are a reasonably prosperous agricultural sector, at least a moderate urban character and some regional market proximity.

For the meat products industry (SIC 201), the only necessary factor appears to be *urban orientation*. And *agricultural prosperity* correlates favorably with the girls', children's, and infants' outerwear (SIC 236) while *regional market proximity* is significant, but negative. The latter means that counties some distance from metropolitan centers should consider this industry a good prospect, and conversely.

106

TABLE 11   Significant Average Factor Score Differences Between Counties Containing and Counties Not Containing Activity in Major Growth Industries in Nonmetropolitan Georgia, 1969

SIC Code	Number of Counties	Dimensions of Socioeconomic Structure					
		Urban orientation	Labor availability	Agricultural prosperity	Regional market proximity	Population age	Manufacturing growth
Prime Growth Industries							
227	20	0.5203	1.2222	0.5636	0.4206		
379	42	0.8257	0.5053			0.3219	
234	24	0.6378	0.7604				
226	9	0.5610	-0.8298		0.5027		
344	43	1.0933					
231	17	0.8531			-0.4246		
238	14	0.9204	-0.5008	0.4366			
329	17				0.4079		
222	9	0.4545	-0.7105				
335	6		-0.7163	0.4264			
282	8	0.6255	-0.5608				0.4691
371	23	0.8123					
364	5						
355	19	0.8493	-0.5312				
Sustained Growth Industries							
232	68		-0.3482		-0.3486	0.4142	
228	31	0.7327	-0.7263	0.3901	0.2884		
201	80	0.8073					
233	43	0.3479					
229	18	0.7295	-0.8113				
251	60	0.8098					
Secondary Growth Industries							
207	21		0.7455				-0.4709
352	27	0.7231	0.4185				
358	8	0.7083			0.9331		
307	14	0.7296					
332	10	1.1696					
264	8	0.8265	-0.6562		0.4079		
236	11			0.4526	-0.5634		
361	3	0.8369					
353	9						
265	11	1.0641	-0.7012				
369	5				0.6136		
319	3	1.0686	-1.3739	1.1385			

SOURCE: Ronald J. Swager, "Locational Requirements of Selected Industries in Nonmetropolitan Areas," AIDC Journal, vol. XII, October 1977, pp. 18–19.

FIG. 13 Site selection checklist. (SOURCE: *Factory Management and Maintenance*, May 1957, pp. 180+. Reprinted by permission of Morgan-Gampion Company.)

	Importance	Site
20. Community Business Climate		
Is attitude of local officials sympathetic and enthusiastic towards existing and new industry?	☐	☐
Is record of local government good as to honesty, efficiency, and principles?	☐	☐
Does community have one or more good business-sponsored civic organizations devoted to improving business climate?	☐	☐
If so, have tangible results been achieved?	☐	☐
If more than one such organization, do they work together harmoniously?	☐	☐
Have you checked reaction of local industries as to business climate?	☐	☐
Have any manufacturers migrated from the community recently?	☐	☐
It is reasonable to expect normal industrial growth in the community?	☐	☐
Are there existing or new industries in the community that help contribute to a stabilized economy?	☐	☐
Is community well diversified industrially?	☐	☐
Are community's industries dynamic and growing?	☐	☐
Is size of community geared to your needs (quantity and quality of industrial neighbors, labor pool, etc.)?	☐	☐
21. Planning and Zoning		
Does community have an active and forward-looking city planning commission?	☐	☐
Are smoke, noise, odors, etc. controlled?	☐	☐
Have zoning sights been properly set in connection with new Federal Highway Programs?	☐	☐

	Importance	Site
Can you expect protection against undesirable neighbors?	☐	☐
Have building codes been adapted to newer "permissive" basis?	☐	☐
Do building inspectors have a reputation for honesty and integrity?	☐	☐

22. Commercial Services

	Importance	Site
Does community contain a diversified amount of commercial services required by industry? (Check and evaluate separately):		
Major repair shops	☐	☐
Electric motor maintenance	☐	☐
Industrial distributors	☐	☐
Lubricants	☐	☐
Lumber and allied materials	☐	☐
Engineering department supplies	☐	☐
Stationery	☐	☐
Food and sundry vending	☐	☐
Local trucking	☐	☐
Railway express	☐	☐
Air freight services	☐	☐
Postal service	☐	☐
Blueprint service	☐	☐
Industrial repair	☐	☐
Air conditioning service	☐	☐
Janitorial service	☐	☐
Professional service	☐	☐
Testing labs	☐	☐
Are adequate construction services and facilities available, either in the community or near it? (Check and evaluate separately):		
Architects	☐	☐
Engineers	☐	☐
Prime contractors	☐	☐
Subcontractors	☐	☐

FIG. 13 (*Continued*)

	Importance	*Site*
Mechanical	☐	☐
Electrical	☐	☐
Piping	☐	☐
Carpenter	☐	☐
Labor	☐	☐
Rigger	☐	☐
Special equipment	☐	☐
Mason	☐	☐
Plasterer	☐	☐
Tile	☐	☐
Painting	☐	☐
Landscape	☐	☐
Paving	☐	☐
Do specialized shops exist in or near the community which can help maintain your special equipment?	☐	☐

23. Community Employer Evaluation	*Importance*	*Site*
Have most employers demonstrated enlightened management policies?	☐	☐
Do branch plants of the community represent national concerns with progressive management-labor-community policies?	☐	☐
Have employers kept pace on a voluntary basis with rising wage standards?	☐	☐
Do you rate the effective level of plant communications between employer and employee to be at least at a satisfactory standard?	☐	☐
Will community progress along lines of guaranteed annual wage fit your proposed wage picture?	☐	☐
Do employers willingly exchange data concerning labor contracts and wages?	☐	☐
Are industrial leaders (and business leaders in		

	Importance	Site
general) active in promoting a better business climate for the community and the state?	☐	☐
Do industrial leaders know and cooperate with local reporters, editors, and radio or TV commentators and program directors?	☐	☐

24. Management Potential

Can prospective workers be expected to grow into added responsibilities?	☐	☐
Can you translate evaluation into estimates for potential supervisors and executives?	☐	☐
Can you expect to recruit certain management echelons locally?	☐	☐
Are specialized skills available, such as scientific and technical manpower?	☐	☐
Have local people responded well to in-plant training?		

From the industrial decision makers' standpoint, among the clear messages, we believe, are that each industry does have specific needs and that locations vary considerably in their ability to meet them. Moreover, the presence of a thriving competitor may be an important indication that a location has those factors you will need for growth, and vice versa. Again, the searcher's first requirements when considering a relocation or expansion are to determine why and what, and then address the question of where.

NOTES

1. *The Community in America*, 2d ed., Rand McNally & Co., Chicago, 1972, p. 27.

111

2. Wolfgang Quante, *The Exodus of Corporate Headquarters from New York City*, Praeger, New York, 1976.

3. William K. MacReynolds, *Contributions to the Theory of Industrial Location: Urban Decentralization*, Ph.D. dissertation, University of Southern California, 1974.

4. James H. Boykin, *Industrial Location Influences Within the Baltimore Region*, Ph.D. dissertation, The American University, 1971.

5. Peter A. Morrison, "Urban Growth and Decline: San Jose and St. Louis in the 1960's." *Science*, vol. 185, August 30, 1974, pp. 757–762. (Copyright 1974 by The American Association for The Advancement of Science.)

6. William C. Wheaton, *Income and Urban Location*, Ph.D. dissertation, University of Pennsylvania, 1972.

7. Marilyn Chase, "The Haight-Ashbury Turns Into a Bastion of the Middle Class," *The Wall Street Journal*, July 24, 1978, pp. 1, 19.

8. Gurney Breckenfeld, "Business Loves the Sunbelt (and Vice Versa)," *Fortune*, June 1977, pp. 132–146.

9. Thomas D. Pearson, *Factors Which Influence the Location of Manufacturing in the Nonmetropolitan United States*, Ph.D. dissertation, Georgia State University, 1974.

10. Ronald J. Dorf, *An Analysis of Manufacturing Location Factors for Communities 2,500 to 50,000 Population in the West North Central Region*, Ph.D. dissertation, Kansas State University, 1975.

11. William F. Davidge, Jr., *The Attractive Influence and Current Adequacy of Mississippi Industrial Location Factors, 1963–1972*, Ph.D. dissertation, The University of Mississippi, 1976.

12. Ralph R. Triplette, Jr., *One-Industry Towns: Their Location, Development and Economic Character*, Ph.D. dissertation, The University of North Carolina at Chapel Hill, 1974.

13. Gurney Breckenfeld, *Columbia and the New Cities*, Ives Washburn, Inc., New York, p. 6.

14. Ibid., pp. 172–173.
15. Ibid., pp. 257–258.
16. Ronald J. Swager, "Locational Requirements of Selected Industries in Nonmetropolitan Areas," *AIDC Journal*, vol. XII, no. 4, October, 1 pp. 7–28. (Article based on the author's doctoral dissertation, *Factors Associated With Industrial Growth in Nonmetropolitan Illinois, Georgia and Ohio, 1959–1969*, University of Illinois, 1975.)

EIGHT

Weighing
the Intangibles

With the stressful situations involved in a relocation, location decision makers need to place added weight on quality-of-life factors. When managers and their families have trouble adjusting to a new community, and the new job also proves unusually hard and frustrating, the manager may solve the problem by changing companies.

Liking the new location better than the old one tops the list of factors that predict whether a manager will be happy after a transfer. The other significant variables, in order of importance, are the adjustment of the spouse, the standard of living, and the number of previous transfers.

A statistical analysis of major determinants of why the new location was preferred provides additional insights. As can be seen in Table 12, city size dominated all other factors studied. Next, the managers (predominately male) placed high value on the city's climate, crime rate, restaurants, and health care facilities. The spouses were more concerned with the cost of living (especially of housing), the availability of housing, and the cultural environment.

TABLE 12   Predictors of Preferences for New versus
Former Location

Urban characteristics	Employees' beta*	Spouses' beta*
Size of city	0.48	0.39
Crime rate	0.27	0.07
Climate	0.24	0.16
Physical surroundings (of the city)	0.20	0.25
Restaurants	0.17	0.13
Local government	0.16	0.12
Medical/health facilities	0.15	0.13
Cost of housing	0.15	0.24
Availability of housing	0.14	0.22
Sports and recreation opportunities	0.13	0.02
Radio/television stations	0.12	0.12
Cost of food	0.11	0.11
Cultural environment	0.10	0.18
Overall cost of living	0.05	0.21
Public transportation	0.05	0.04
Enviromental quality (pollution)	0.01	0.08

*A measure of the ability of the predictor to explain variation in the dependent variable after adjusting for the effects of all other predictors.

SOURCE: Adapted from Table 5, p. 553, Craig C. Pinder, "Multiple Predictors of Post-Transfer Satisfaction: The Role of Urban Factors," *Personnel Psychology*, vol. 30, 1977.

But as Craig C. Pinder of the University of British Columbia (Vancouver) points out, city size does not necessarily mean that large cities are preferred over small ones but rather that other dimensions tend to correlate with physical size. "Companies might be well advised," he observes, "to assure that the transfers they impose on their transferees do not entail real decreases in either standard of living or status in the organization, if they want to assure favorable transfer-related attitudes among their employees."[1]

Performance remains a function of both ability and motivation. "Consequently, managers with demonstrated ability will not achieve expected results in a new plant if their environment creates dissatisfactions that adversely affect motivation," notes Kurt R. Student.

Student, a management psychologist for Rohrer, Hibler & Replogle, Inc., observes that while the majority of the work force may come from the immediate area, the success of the new plant largely depends on the new facility's management team, who are usually transferees.

"*People* make organizations work, not vice versa," stresses Dr. Student. "I thoroughly endorse the goal of profit maximization in plant location, but I question whether this goal can be achieved by most current decision processes which exclude nonquantitative, intangible quality of life considerations."[2]

THE TRANSFER BLUES

Relocation can be an extremely stressful event. Taking place within a relatively brief time period, it involves the whole family. For the transferring employee, the most important factor throughout is the job, and moving usually means a promotion, more pay, and more responsibility, or at the least a change which will broaden work skills and lead to more pay, a promotion, etc. Spouses whose career concerns are less paramount usually have more of a need for community integration. A move means leaving their friends and starting again from scratch socially and in local organizations. Children also generally prefer stability to change and uncertainty.[3]

Table 13 summarizes the factors that can create or relieve the stressful conditions where a move involves a male manager and his wife. In this situation, the man not only has to conquer the nearly overwhelming demands of the new job,

TABLE 13 Factors Which Accentuate or Attenuate the Stress Involved in Moving for the Manager and His Wife

	The Manager	
Before the Move	During the Move	After the Move

Before the Move	During the Move	After the Move
MINUS	**MINUS**	**MINUS**
Happy in previous job	Extra physical demands of travel and extra work	New Job makes excessive demands
Reservations about new job (e.g., lateral transfer, no salary increase)	House hunting is difficult and uncertain	Interpersonal problems at work
Doubts ability to master new job	Has to travel on business at time of move	Lacks skills new job requires
Wife reluctant to move (e.g., leaving friends or her job)	Separation	Needs to prove himself quickly
Children at important stage of education	Wife and children unhappy at his absence	Worried that unable to afford new mortgage
Family regard present area as home	Wife jealous of his freedom from responsibility	Concerned because wife and children having problems adapting
Worried about effects on wife and children	Finds it difficult to balance competing demands on his time and interest	Area doesn't offer desired facilities (e.g., sports)
PLUS	**PLUS**	**PLUS**
Happy about new job (if was for promotion, etc.)	Enjoys freedom and "bachelor" social life	Job goes well and is satisfying
Loss of motivation for previous job	Involved in new job	New work team provide support
Wife eager to move	House transactions accomplished relatively easily and quickly	Family adapt relatively easily
The move brings benefits to the family (a new house, better schooling)	Makes money on the exchange	

118

The Manager's Wife

MINUS	MINUS	MINUS
Dislikes upheaval and change	Has to cope with a lot of extra work	Feels lonely and isolated (misses old friends and doesn't make new ones)
Involved in local community	Misses husband	Locals are hostile to strangers
Likes current house	Finds she has little social support in the area	New house unsatisfactory or needs tiring alterations
Works outside the home	Feels that husband does not appreciate her problems, is jealous of his freedom	Dislikes characteristics of the area
Children at critical stage of education	Children upset and miss their father	Husband too involved in new job to give support
Children reluctant to move or react badly to change (she worries about their ability to cope)	House hunting and timing of move are uncertain and exhausting	No job opportunities for her
Lives near her parents		Lives further away from parents
		Children have problems at school (slow to make new friends)
		Husband unhappy in new job
PLUS	**PLUS**	**PLUS**
Dislikes current situation (geographic area, house etc.)	Friends rally round	Befriended by neighbor or company wife
Enjoys change and seeing new places	Separation kept to a minimum by easy transactions, etc.	Already has friends in the area
Likes proposed new location (has friends there)	Finds she can cope and takes pride in her new independence	Makes friends via established channels (the church, baby-sitting club, etc.)
Children will benefit (better quality schooling; can start again if problems at school or with social lives)		Husband and children adapt easily and quickly
		Moves nearer to parents

SOURCE: Cary L. Cooper & Judi Marshall, *Understanding Executive Stress*, PBI Books, New York, 1977, pp. 128–129.

he also has additional responsibilities such as finding a suitable house in a suitable neighborhood. A hotel room often becomes home for four to five nights a week. Meantime, the wife has to assume his normal chores as well as her own and be both father and mother to the children while arranging the sale of the current house. Then on the weekends, when both are tired and exhausted from the extra demands of the week, they must face and solve mutual problems. As a result, relocation can be a major strain on even the best of relationships.

Obviously, the importance of major relocation problems varies with one's marital state and ages of any children. While married couples with young children have the most problems, older couples may have special concerns such as the care of a parent.

More and more male executives have wives who also want satisfying work, observe Cary L. Cooper, Professor of Management Education at the University of Manchester Institute of Science and Technology, and Judi Marshall, on the teaching staff of the same university. While the husband's within-company transfer means another step on the corporate ladder, the wife must usually start again from scratch in the new location.

> Relocation means a disruptive end and a traumatic beginning. If she adds mother to her repertoire of roles, the manager's wife stands even less chance of achieving any work ambitions she may have. . . . As men and women experiment with their own and each other's roles, the balance of power is shifting, not only within the family, but also within the companies which employ its members. Male members seem to be setting themselves lower ambitions, while their wives strive to fill three highly demanding roles simultaneously.[4]

RELOCATION DETERRENTS

According to Dr. Weston E. Edwards, chairman and chief executive officer of Merrill Lynch Relocation Management Inc., a background study of company moves concluded that the largest sector of the United States economy, manufacturing companies, did not transfer any more employees in 1977 than in 1972. The service sector, however, has been increasing its transfers considerably. As a result, the total number of people being moved each year continues to range from 200,000 to 300,000. Says Edwards:

> The foremost deterrent to relocation that we have found is the women's movement—the wife is just not as willing as she used to be to transfer. In fact, she now more frequently has a job equally important to her as her husband's is to him, and is therefore concerned about how she will find employment at the new location.
>
> Secondly, there is the increased divergence of home values from one city to another. Naturally employees and their families do not want to move and have a drop in their standard of living—and that is what many moves today threaten to do. For example, a $50,000 home in Columbus, Ohio, may require $150,000 in Newport Beach, California.
>
> Thirdly, we find employees simply putting a higher value on the quality of their present lives—what now brings them pleasure—than on higher pay and greater promotional opportunity, when that requires being uprooted again.[5]

Merrill Lynch suggests several ways to surmount the increasing reluctance of employees to move: more liberal house-hunting trips, job-finding assistance for the spouse, full relocation benefits for new-hires, mortgage and equity loan financing assistance, cost-of-living differentials, and an offer to move the family back to the former location if after

121

a year the transfer is unsuccessful. Companies should send the employee's spouse on that first job evaluation trip to get a feel for the available housing and job opportunities. And although companies have not yet adopted a formal policy of job assistance for the employee's spouse, Merrill Lynch believes this is an area in which more will need to be done in the future.

Another part of the problem, the company notes, is that the prices of homes in the $100,000-plus bracket—the level sought by many executives—have been escalating at 12 to 15 percent a year since the mid-1970s, as compared with about 7 percent annually for lower priced homes.

Employers should recognize that the greater emphasis on the quality of life and the increased number of women in the work force with jobs that they enjoy, means a company "should not assume that employees will still jump when they whistle, in this or any other area, and *should* anticipate possible rejection of even the most attractive offer," suggests Dr. J. H. Foegen, Professor of Business at Winona State University (Winona, Minnesota).

"Many of today's upper-level managers . . . have been used to subordinates [who have accepted] direction without question. . . . Relocation that appears very attractive to a superior—perhaps partly for selfish reasons—might be less so to the person directly involved."[6]

"Contrary to conventional wisdom which tells that men and women can learn to like almost anything," adds Dr. Student, "dissatisfactions with community life remain salient for years. Dissatisfaction with schools, housing and community services receive almost daily reinforcement; consequently, these dissatisfactions do not go away easily."[7]

What is this elusive condition that relocation specialists and others refer to as *quality of life?*

Basically, it is the interests of people. Dr. Student has identified five primary factors: social-cultural, medical, educational, political, and residential.

Social-cultural refers to access to network and educational television and to the availability of good restaurants, theater, concerts, and other activities the transferee and family could attend. There should be a library with business reference materials. Good transportation with access to an airport that connects easily with major cities certainly makes life more pleasant for the manager not privileged to use the corporate airplane. And finally, how far will the location be from major sporting events and from live theater and other artistic programs of high quality?

As for health care, a community should have complete primary medical care (general medicine, general surgery, pediatrics, and gynecology and obstetrics) services, with specialized care available within a reasonable distance. [8] A hospital with emergency services is a must for possible industrial accidents as well as for the general welfare of all community members. The ages of the local physicans can also be important. If all are very near retirement age, the future of the health care of the community could be in jeopardy.

The quality of education and the local and state tax base usually have a direct correlation: low taxes, poor education. Families that are not satisfied with the educational standards of their communities can experience a high degree of stress and tension. Particularly affected are those parents who plan to send their children to college when few native families have similar aspirations for their children. Graduation from a high school not noted for its academic standards can make it difficult for the children of the middle management executive to gain admission to a top-ranking college.

The political climate of a small town can also create frustrations for the public-minded executive. In one-party towns run by native families, there usually are few opportunities for an "outsider" to participate actively in any meaningful role.

Finally, small towns can lack sufficient rental housing and supply of older homes or new homes available for occupancy. New homes are built only on demand and force the family to choose between a house far below their accustomed standards or face a six-month or more separation while the new home is built. Another problem common to small towns can be that the new company's executives all wind up living in the same area of town and often are close neighbors. As a result, the manager seldom has an opportunity to escape totally from the problems of the job, and the manager's family members may have to walk on eggs to keep from offending the boss's family.

In-depth interviews with twenty-eight residential housing developers in the Atlanta metropolitan area found three location factors of top importance when selecting land: highway access, proximity to schools, and availability of public utilities.[9] Proximity to shopping and topographic factors were also frequently mentioned. The interviewees indicated their perception of factors home buyers consider important are (from greatest to least): lot factors, utility and service factors, social factors, neighborhood factors, dwelling factors, financial factors, and accessibility factors.

SUGGESTED GUIDELINES

When a new plant runs into trouble, states Dr. Student, it's usually the human factors that are the culprit. To avoid that happening, he offers these suggestions:

1. Make sure that a personnel specialist or consultant contributes to the site selection deliberations. Require reports on the social-cultural, medical, educational, political, and residential characteristics of the proposed community.

2. After selecting a site, have the prospective managers and their spouses meet with the specialist and get their response. Then arrange a company-sponsored visit to the community by the manager and spouse.

3. Offer the manager the job only if *both* the manager and spouse react favorably to the transfer.

"I would make a final and admittedly controversial recommendation," adds Dr. Student. "I believe that a 'critical mass' in population is necessary before you can expect a community to meet the requirements I've set." He suggests that the critical mass is "about 10,000 people," and that ideally the community should be within one hour's easy drive from a major metropolitan center.[10]

FIG. 14   Site selection checklist. (SOURCE: *Factory Management and Maintenance*, May 1957, pp. 180+. Reprinted by permission of Morgan-Gampion Company.)

25. General Community Aspects	Importance	Site
Is physical appearance of center of town a pleasant one?	☐	☐
Are there good hotels, motels, restaurants?	☐	☐
Are shopping and commercial districts well laid out for parking facilities and easy flow of traffic?	☐	☐
To ease parking problems, are there fringe parking areas coupled with transit facilities?	☐	☐
Are there adequate local banking facilities?	☐	☐

FIG. 14   (*Continued*)

	Importance	Site
26. Maturity of Citizens		
Do local civic and religious leaders have enlightened and progressive attitude toward business and industry (public, civic, commercial, religious, news, etc.)?	☐	☐
Do people of community display political awareness?	☐	☐
How many voters went to the polls in the last municipal election?	☐	☐
How many voters went to the polls in the last national election?	☐	☐
Do local people understand how business operates in the American economy?	☐	☐
Do local citizens really encourage new industry?	☐	☐
Are there community educational programs directed at young people?	☐	☐
Do social and economic backgrounds of community point toward maturity?	☐	☐
Is standard of living at or above the national average?		
27. Residental Housing		
Are there enough rental properties for new employees?	☐	☐
Are there plenty of houses available in the several cost brackets that will appeal to new salaried employees?	☐	☐
Are there attractive suburbs within convenient distance of selected community?	☐	☐
Are community housing starts keeping up with expected growth?	☐	☐
As one index of community values, are residential property values increasing in line with area averages?	☐	☐

	Importance	Site
Is over-all impression of residential areas an attractive one?	☐	☐
Is community saddled with submarginal or slum areas?	☐	☐
If so, are clearance and rehabilitation plans progressing?	☐	☐
Does extent of home ownership among hourly type of employee indicate stability and community pride?	☐	☐

28. Education

	Importance	Site
Are there sufficient schools, and adequately staffed?	☐	☐
Is school building program in keeping with forecast community growth?	☐	☐
What about vocational, trade, and apprentice training opportunities? Are they oriented toward your requirements?	☐	☐
Do any institutions offer foremanship courses?	☐	☐
Are college facilities near enough for offering special courses to key personnel?	☐	☐
Are there adult education programs? Do they offer degrees?	☐	☐
Is educational picture above average in terms of expense per pupil, teachers' salaries, PTA enthusiasm, building programs, etc.?	☐	☐

29. Health and Welfare

	Importance	Site
Are there satisfactory medical and health services?	☐	☐
Hospitals? General practitioners?	☐	☐
How about auxiliary medical services? (dentists, visiting nurses, clinics, etc.)	☐	☐
Do hospitals have adequate ratings by State Board of Health?	☐	☐

FIG. 14   (*Continued*)

	Importance	Site
How large an area is served by hospitals?	☐	☐
Are Blue Cross and allied plans available?	☐	☐
Does community have a workable disaster plan?	☐	☐
Is there an adequate public health program?	☐	☐
Is community welfare and relief load in reasonable proportion to that of area?	☐	☐
Does community participate actively and responsibly in community fund program?	☐	☐
Does the community have adequate and well-enforced sanitary laws?	☐	☐
Are there reasonable state industrial and health laws?	☐	☐

30. Culture and Recreation

	Importance	Site
Are there a variety of local outdoors attractions? (For example: golf, tennis, swimming, boating, fishing, hunting, skating, skiing.)	☐	☐
What about family recreational areas? Parks and playgrounds?	☐	☐
Is community near to good resort areas?	☐	☐
Are there sufficient number of places of worship of varying denominations?	☐	☐
Are there adequately staffed and equipped libraries?	☐	☐
Are quality and variety of fraternal organizations attractive to potential newcomers?	☐	☐
Do civic attractions operate, such as museums, theater, and musical functions?	☐	☐
Are there a variety of paid amusements?	☐	☐
What facilities are there for public gatherings, such as public buildings, auditoriums, gymnasiums, and church edifices?	☐	☐
Is there an active press, including dailies, weeklies, radio, and TV?	☐	☐

NOTES

1. Craig C Pinder, "Multiple Predictors of Post-Transfer Satisfaction: The Role of Urban Factors," *Personnel Psychology*, vol. 30, 1977, pp. 543–546.

2. Kurt R. Student, "Cost vs. Human Values in Plant Location," *Business Horizons*, April 1976, pp. 5–14.

3. Cary L. Cooper & Judi Marshall, *Understanding Executive Stress*, PBI Books, New York, 1977, "Stressful Events: A Case Study of the Mobile Manager and His Wife." pp. 120–154.

4. Ibid., pp. 153–154.

5. Weston E. Edwards, "Prescriptions for Relocation Policy . . . Coping with the Forces of Change," *Proceedings of Relocation Management '78*, Merrill Lynch Relocation Management Inc., pp. 51–65.

6. J. H. Foegen, "If It Means Moving, Forget It!," *Personnel Journal*, August 1977, pp. 414–416.

7. Kurt R. Student, op. cit., p. 7.

8. "Don't Forget the 'People Factor'," *Industry Week*, April 21, 1975, pp. 62–63.

9. Kenneth B. Kenney, *The Residential Land Developer and his Land Purchase Decision*, Ph.D. dissertation, University of North Carolina at Chapel Hill, 1972.

10. "Don't Forget the 'People Factor'," op. cit.

NINE

Finding
the Financing

Wisconsin's Office of State Planning and Energy, Department of Administration, recently commissioned a study of the business loan programs of 26 states. Among the findings: States with a strong manufacturing sector and/or high corporate taxes tended to have a business loan program or guarantee program; states with high property taxes or budget surpluses were not as likely to have a loan program or loan guarantees.[1]

Most states help finance the building and construction of facilities, the purchase of machinery and equipment, and the acquisition of land through state loan guarantee programs. These aim at the same needs and assure the lender that the major portion of the long-term loan will be repaid by either the borrower or by the state. The state charges the lender a small fee for this guarantee.

Seventeen of the twenty-six states studied administer a direct loan program, with three more poised to provide one. Fifteen states offer a loan guarantee, with New York state moving toward adoption. Six states now offer both programs in some form, and three more may soon have both. Table 14 summarizes the survey results.

Whatever the loan form, the purposes remain basically the same—to ease unemployment, to enhance the prospects for increased business activity, to encourage business diversification, and to ensure extension of existing credit lines. Table 15 provides some additional details on the lending activity; the last column shows both the number and type of loans. The legal lending limits within the states for particular types of loans are shown in Table 16.

As they are intended to be, manufacturing firms are the principal users of state business loans or guarantees although other business can often obtain state help if the

TABLE 14   Loan Program Available from Certain States [a]

State	Direct loan			Loan Guarantee		
	Building and construction	Machinery and equipment	Other	Building and construction	Machinery and equipment	Other
Alaska	X [b]	X				
Arkansas				X	X	
Connecticut	X	X	A, B	X	X	
Delaware	X	X	A, B	X	X	
Hawaii	X	X	A, B, C			
Illinois	X		A			
Indiana				X	X	A, C, J
Kentucky	X		D			
Maine				X	X	
Maryland				X	X	A, I
Massachusetts				X	X	A, B, I
Michigan	X	X		X	X	
Minnesota	X	X	A, E, F	X	X	A

132

TABLE 14   *(Continued)*

State	Direct loan			Loan Guarantee		
	Building and construction	Machinery and equipment	Other	Building and construction	Machinery and equipment	Other
Missouri	X*	X	C, G			
New Hampshire	X°	X°		X	X	
New Jersey		X	C, G, H		X	C, G, H
New York	X	X	I	X°ᵈ	X°ᵈ	
North Dakota*	X	X	C			
Ohio	X°ᵈ			X	X	
Oklahoma	X	X	A			
Pennsylvania	X		A			
Rhode Island				Xᶠ	Xᶠ	A
Tennessee	X°	X°		X	X	
Texas	X	X				
Vermont	X	X		X	X	
West Virginia	X		A			

"Table symbols:
A = real estate
B = pollution control
C = working capital
D = purchase, development of industrial subdivisions
E = technical assistance
F = feasibility studies
G = inventory
H = expansion and conversion
I = rehabilitation
J = accounts receivable
X = active program
X° = program is authorized but inactive
ᵇNot encouraged
ᶜIncludes site development and interim construction financing
ᵈInactive only because implementing legislation has not yet been passed
ᵉBank of North Dakota is the only state-owned bank in USA. Its Commercial Loan Dept. administers a program in which the Bank (1) participates in loans of all kinds and (2) purchases the guaranteed portions of SBA and FMHA loans.
ᶠThis program currently applies only to *new* building and construction and *new* machinery and equipment.

SOURCE: Jack R. Huddleston and Doris L. Fischer, *Preliminary Economic Research On a State Business Loan Program: Final Report*, Wisconsin Office of State Planning & Energy, Department of Administration, June 30, 1978.

TABLE 15 The Number and Types of Loans Provided by Certain States

State	Direct loans outstanding	Loan guarantees outstanding	Guarantee limits	Gross direct activity figures (No. of projects/total loan value)
Alaska	$39 million, after 1st 8 mo., fiscal year (FY) 78			**FY 73 to 1st 8 mo. of FY 78, 667; loan value $64.8 mill.**
Arkansas		$19 million	$25 mill.	
Connecticut	$25 million	$73 million	$140 mill.	
Delaware	$140.7 million	$34.6 million	$50 mill.	40
Hawaii	$3.6 mill., 12/31/77			262/$7.5 million
Illinois	$1.04 million			36/$1.8 million
Indiana		$1.7 million	Each $1 mill. can be leveraged 4X	
Kentucky	$10 million			71/$7.9 million*
Maine		$21 million	$80 million-industrial† $17 million-recreational	80 industrial, $66 million 35 recreational, $16 million
Maryland		$29 million	not more than 5× reserve fund	

			$9 insurance for every $1 in reserve fund	
Massachusetts		too early		
Michigan		too early		
Minnesota	$1.25 million	$3,400	5× development revenue fund	~59
Missouri	$3.3 million			14/$4 million
New Hampshire	<$700,000‡		$20 million§	11 industrial, $4.2 million / 5 recreational, $900,000
New Jersey			$10 million	20
New York				total loans/713 $95 million
North Dakota	$79 million (partic. loans) $11.9 million(SBA loans)			on hand: 668(partic. loans) 98(SBA loans)
Ohio		$8.5 million	$54 million	
Oklahoma				currently, 110 active loans
Pennsylvania	$350 million			1418 as of 12/31/76 $429 million
Rhode Island		$45 million	$80 million	
Tennessee		$750,000	$30 million	

TABLE 15 (Continued)

State	Direct loans outstanding	Loan guarantees outstanding	Guarantee limits	Gross direct activity figures (No. of projects/total loan value)
Texas				7
Vermont	$4.2 million, current	$26.2 million, current	$3.5 million	as of 6/30/77/22 $2.8 million
West Virginia	$6.5 million			90

*industrial subdivision   19
building & construction $\underline{52}$
   71 loans

†MGA cannot guarantee > $2.5 million per year.
‡Plus a lease-purchase arrangement of $400,000.
§industrial

machinery and equipment $15 million
recreation   3
   $\underline{2}$
   $20 million

building & construction $20
machinery and equipment $\underline{15}$
   $35 million

SOURCE: Jack R. Huddleston and Doris L. Fischer, *Preliminary Economic Research On a State Business Loan Program: Final Report*, Wisconsin Office of State Planning & Energy, Department of Administration, June 30, 1978.

136

TABLE 16 The Legal Lending Limits for Certain States

State	Percent of project costs loan can cover			Percent of loan guarantee can cover		
	Building and construction	Machinery and equipment	Other	Building and construction	Machinery and equipment	Other
Alaska	75%	75%				
Arkansas				100%	100%	
Connecticut	90%	80% †	80% Pollution control	90%	80%	
Delaware	100%	100%		100%	100%	
Hawaii	90%‡	90%	90%			
Illinois	30%					
Indiana				90%	75%	75%
Kentucky	50%		industrial 40%-subdiv			
Maine				90%-ind.	75%-ind.	75%-recr.
Maryland				90%	70%	
Massachusetts				40%	40%	40%

137

TABLE 16 *(Continued)*

State	Percent of project costs loan can cover			Percent of loan guarantee can cover		
	Building and construction	Machinery and equipment	Other	Building and construction	Machinery and equipment	Other
Michigan	90%	90%.		90%	90%	
Minnesota	20%	20%		20%	20%	
Missouri	50% match of bank's loan					
New Hampshire	100% *	85%*		30–50 %	35%	
New Jersey		100%	100%		90%	90%
New York	40%	40%		80%*	80%*	
North Dakota	Varies, but no more than 60% of lead fin. inst's. share		All of the 90% portion guaranteed by SBA, FMHA			

138

Ohio	40%*		90%	90%
Oklahoma	25%	25%		
Pennsylvania	40%			
Rhode Island			100%	100%
Tennessee	*		90%	90%
Texas	40%	40%		
Vermont	40%		90%	90%
West Virginia	50%			

*Program is authorized, but inactive.
†Must be in conjunction with building and construction project.
‡Participation loan is preferred.

SOURCE: Jack R. Huddleston and Doris L. Fischer, *Preliminary Economic Research On a State Business Loan Program: Final Report,* Wisconsin Office of State Planning & Energy, Department of Administration, June 30,1978.

proposed project will create new employment or preserve existing jobs. Some states give preferential treatment to small and/or minority firms, and a few consider themselves as the lender of last resort, but the majority do not administer their programs for the benefit of any particular economic segment. As a rule of thumb, direct loans average $100,000 to $500,000, while loan guarantees generally fall into the $250,000 to $800,000 range.

ONE STATE'S PROGRAM

The state of Maryland's industrial financing programs will serve again as our in-depth example of how a state will work with industry.

Industrial financing is available from many private, public, and quasi-public sources in Maryland:

Maryland Industrial Development Financing Authority (MIDFA) can insure mortgages for real estate up to 90 percent, and for machinery and equipment up to 70 percent. Limited to manufacturing, research and development facilities, corporate headquarters and regional office buildings, and pollution control facilities, interest on the loans may be exempt from income tax (pursuant to Internal Revenue Service regulations).

Industrial Revenue Bonds are issued by counties in Maryland: 100 percent financing coverage for real estate and for machinery and equipment is possible (same limitations as above); subject to IRS regulations, the bonds can be issued at tax exempt rates.

Development Credit Corporation (DCC) may grant loans to cover 100 percent of cost but usually keeps its involvement to 50 percent or less. Any business or industrial enterprise unable to obtain funds from conventional sources can apply; the interest charged cannot exceed 4 percent over the prime rate prevailing in the city of Baltimore on unsecured commercial loans.

Maryland Area Redevelopment Act provides matching funds with communities for the financing of Economic Development Administration (EDA) projects to a maximum of 5 percent of the total cost. The interest rate charged by the state is limited to 4 percent.

Local Development Organizations within local communities may assist in the financing of industrial projects in conjunction with EDA and the Small Business Administration.

General Obligation Bonds can be issued to finance industrial projects by counties in which acute unemployment exists.

Banks and Insurance Companies participate in many of the previously listed programs as well as provide direct loans through normal business channels.

We will consider the first three of these financing programs.

MIDFA

The Maryland Industrial Development Financing Authority is a unit of the Maryland Department of Economic and Community Development. It was established in 1965 "for the purpose of facilitating the financing of business enterprises seeking to locate or expand their operations in the State." By insuring loans made by private lenders such as commercial banks, insurance companies, savings and loan associations, etc., MIDFA usually enables borrowers to obtain loans at a higher percentage of project cost than available conventionally and at interest costs at generally two percent or more below conventional rates. Land, buildings, and equipment can be financed through this program.

By Maryland law, the political subdivision (almost always the county) obtains the loan with the company as the lessee and MIDFA as guarantor. The lender and MIDFA agree on the allocation of the potential liability in the event of business failure or lease default. Once the loan is paid, the property is then conveyed by the political subdivision to the company for a nominal amount (usually $1 or $10).

The lender, says John G. Fitzpatrick, Deputy Director of MIDFA, looks at five benchmarks when evaluating a loan application: (1) strength of the credit, (2) size of the loan, (3) term of the loan—the longer the term the higher the rate, (4) ease with which the loan is "booked" (structured), and (5) importance of a customer or potential customer.

How does one go about choosing a lender? Fitzpatrick suggests that you do it the way you would any other potential partner in business. Ask your local bank to recommend several in the community under consideration, write for their annual reports directly, or through a surrogate, and study them. One point you should note is the bank's tax bracket. Most larger banks have a 25 to 27 percent federal tax bracket and *the higher the tax bracket* the lower the rate the bank should quote on the loan. The bank will likely suggest a time period of fifteen to twenty-five years for the loan; the average tax-free loan in Maryland is about twenty years.

Another role MIDFA serves in the loan process is that of Bond Counsel. MIDFA rules on the eligibility of the borrower and whether the loan would serve a public purpose. For this determination, MIDFA can charge an insurance premium of up to 3 percent. In practice, it charges one-half of one percent and automatically waives this fee for economically depressed areas (by definition, one with an unemployment rate of 1 percent or more above the national average). Also, MIDFA normally insures only a portion of the loan to reduce the exposure to normal levels.

Since MIDFA was established, it has approved eighty-two loans with only two defaults. "In the first six months of 1978," adds Fitzpatrick, "MIDFA has cleared 13 loans because people have begun to catch on to what a good deal it can be." Currently, a special program for the small businessperson who needs a loan in the $50,000 to $100,000 range is under consideration.

As observed earlier, MIDFA functions for fixed asset financing and cannot be used for working capital, refinancing, or any other such corporate borrowing need. The legal limit for a loan in Maryland by MIDFA is $5 million. To date, $3.3 million has been the largest loan and $153,000 the smallest (with $120,000 probably the lowest we would go, says Fitzpatrick). The typical loan ranges from $300,000 to $700,000.

"It is very important that no binding commitments to purchase real estate or equipment be made prior to obtaining MIDFA approval," Fitzpatrick told us.

INDUSTRIAL REVENUE BONDS

While the lender in the previous discussion is a private organization, industrial development bonds are sold by a cooperating Maryland county or municipality for a specific industrial or public service company. Payment of the principal and interest is provided by lease rental payments, installment purchase payments, or loan repayments. The legal documents also provide for payment by the lessee of the maintenance and operating expenses of the project being financed and the payment of all applicable taxes, including real estate taxes.

These bonds are exempt from all federal, state and local income taxes and have an upper limit of $10 million. Generally speaking, companies with strong balance sheets usually opt for this route over MIDFA approval with its added insurance cost. For the most part, the total amount to be financed by industrial revenue bonds should be at least $1 million due to fixed costs associated with any bond issue.

DEVELOPMENT CREDIT CORPORATION

Development Credit Corporation of Maryland was created by a special act of the General Assembly in 1959 for the purpose of "stimulating business and industry in the State of Maryland by making loans when and to the extent such loans are not otherwise readily available." All but fourteen states have active programs similar to DCCM, and five of those have authorized such programs although they are currently inactive.

A private company with a state charter, DCCM seeks to help deserving companies that cannot secure a conventional loan from a bank or other traditional lending institution. The firm may not have a sufficient track record to demonstrate adequate cash flow or sufficient collateral to satisfy normal loan requirements. DCCM is not a venture capital firm in the strictest sense; rather, it seeks to loan to fledging companies where some evidence of managerial ability to operate profitably already exists.

DCCM will make loans from $25,000 to $320,000. Unlike MIDFA, the funds can be used for working capital, equipment acquisition, or almost any other financial need. However, DCCM and MIDFA do cooperate when guaranteed loans for fixed assets can be coupled with filling a need for working capital. DCCM has 247 stockholders, including 39 Maryland banks, and makes its profit on the interest spread between what it charges and what it pays for funds.

Most of the loan funds are supplied by the Member Banks. But the Small Business Administration, which has a special program called Section 501 for loans only to state-wide development companies, does supply about a quarter of DCCM's funds. DCCM has to pay the Member Banks and SBA interest.

Most of the applicants for loans are directed to DCCM by a member bank unwilling to extend the kind of credit needed but willing to purchase a small first-out direct participation in any loan that DCCM will make. Typically the first-out will average around 20 percent, although it can range from 10 percent to 50 percent. On April 30, 1978, DCCM's fiscal year, there were fifty-eight loans receivable on its books, spread among forty-five borrowers and totaling close to $7 million. Loans are made at 3 to 4 percent over the prime rate.

NOTES

1. Jack R. Huddleston and Doris L. Fischer, *Preliminary Economic Research on a State Business Loan Program: Final Report*, Wisconsin Office of State Planning and Energy, Department of Administration, June 30, 1978.

145

TEN

Selecting
the Best Site

By this time, the location decision maker should have a clear picture of the "ideal" location, and may even have narrowed the choices to two or three prime sites. The purpose of this and subsequent chapters will be to present some additional data that might be useful in weighing the alternatives.

Throughout the site selection process, the location decision maker will have to pass judgment on the information and advice supplied by a number of specialists. The average project will involve the talents of a planner, an architect, an interior designer, lawyers, and engineers. In addition, help toward problem solving may require experts in materials handling, word processing, communications, data processing, and market research, plus management and methods consultants.

NONMANUFACTURING FACTORS

For office location determinations, the type of business takes on importance. If there is a constant face-to-face dialogue required between employees and customers, then location near an airport and/or interstate highway system may be a prime consideration. On the other hand, if communication takes place chiefly via the telephone and correspondence, then out-of-the-way, and probably relatively inexpensive locations might well meet the need. When large numbers of clerical workers are required, a highly populated area or one near a business district well served by public transportation might be the best choice.

In addition to the accessibility of the site and its environment, don't skimp on the size of the potential site. Particularly in suburban areas, it is important to allow for possible expansion and sufficient parking space. But even in the city, a building just looks better if it has some space around it. And in these days of energy consideration, a poor orientation relative to the sun can mean excessive air conditioning expenses.

Assuming that several potential locations have been selected, the next step would be to call on the city planning commission, urban renewal groups, other firms, and the local Chamber of Commerce in each target area to determine which neighborhoods might be most appropriate for your type of business. Then, the company can list its space and neighborhood requirements with one or more real estate brokers.

As Kenneth H. Ripnen, chief executive architect of Ripnen Architects, P.C., points out,

> Normally before purchase of land an option to buy is negotiated. This is subject to approval and consideration of the following:
>
> Physical—Water supply, gas, electricity, sewage, pedestrian and vehicular circulation systems, land-use, and city planning.

Social—Housing, schools, libraries, city hall, stores, shopping centers, religious buildings, and clubs.

Economics—Police, fire, garbage collection and disposal, community services, and tax base.

Environment—Air, water, and land pollution; e.g., potential traffic pollution of nearby residential areas may result in refusal of a permit to build.[1]

A more detail checklist appears in Figure 15.

For the small business, the choice of location looms even

FIG. 15 **Criteria for evaluation of a specific site.** (SOURCE: Kenneth H. Ripnen, *Office Space Administration*, McGraw-Hill, 1974, p. 174.)

Access
Immediate vicinity
   Street width
   Traffic volumes and characteristics
   Turning movements and signalization
   Parking and other traffic controls
   Public transportation
   Possible access points to site
   Known plans for improvements
Regional (employee and customer- oriented)
   Driving time to population centers
   Road capacity and future highway improvements
   Availability of public transportation

Utilities
Availability and Capacity to Serve the Site
   Water supply
   Storm sewers
   Electricity
   Communications
   Estimated cost and timing for providing same
   Sanitary sewers

FIG. 15 *(Continued)*

Gas
Heating
Site Development Factors
Size
Topography
Drainage
Natural features, vegetation, conservation factors, views,
     appearance
Zoning of site
Condition, utilization of existing buildings
Shape of property
Soils
Tree coverage
Space for expansion

Neighborhood Development Factors
Existing development pattern in the immediate area and
     district/trends
Zoning of the surrounding area
Relationship to community's master plan
Community and neighborhood factors
Availability of supporting commercial and industrial activities
Availability of supporting educational, cultural, and
     recreational activities
Housing

Legal and Other Impediments
Deed restrictions
Easements
Other government programs and restrictions affecting the site
Need for zoning changes

**Legal and Other Impediments, Acquisition Costs for
     Alternative Sites, Timing of Project Development, Other
     Considerations**

---

more important. Small-business tenants often don't realize that many parts of a commercial lease are negotiable. A good broker will try to negotiate favorable terms for tenants on such items as escalation clauses, installation work, take-over of existing lease obligations, moving expenses, and options to expand and/or renew. Small businesses without proper protection in their leases can find themselves moved from floor to floor to accommodate the needs of larger tenants.

Small business can receive some help from the U.S. Census Bureau in obtaining data for making a location decision. The Census Bureau not only provides population figures, information on types of households, and data on the purchasing habits of an area (number of automobiles, appliances, etc.), but also facts on the type and size of competitive businesses in the target area. Details on the various publications available and the data they contain can be acquired by ordering the Bureau of Census Catalog, Superintendent of Documents, Washington, D.C. 20402 (most recent price, $4).

MANUFACTURING CONSIDERATIONS

The chief decision makers of 122 manufacturing plants located in Marion County, Illinois, were surveyed in 1974 by Prentice Knight for his dissertation. The purpose was to determine what location factors manufacturers consider most important when choosing among industrial districts. Most believe that costs vary considerably from district to district but that sales and revenue do not. Thus, the major location factors revolve around the district's internal characteristics rather than its geographical relationship to other points in the urban area. Most frequently mentioned were availability of adequate sites, the difficulty of attracting the needed labor, taxes, the ease of getting trucks in and out, and the "safeness" of an area.

Generally speaking, notes Knight, the decision makers emphasize as factors of importance those most related to the disadvantages of their present location. For example, those with small locally owned factories in the suburbs often seem most concerned with noneconomic problems, such as the travel time to residence.[2]

When choosing among sites within a region, analysis has shown that plants place greatest importance on access to interstate highways, access to commercial airports, and the presence of sewer systems serving the site. The importance of the last two increases with plant employment size, observes Eugene Gishlick. For his doctoral thesis he looked at why fifty-five plant sites were chosen over alternative sites and found that the larger the proposed employment of a plant, the smaller the size of the community chosen. Plants with large employment tended to seek smaller communities in the vicinity of metropolitan labor markets, while smaller plants tended to locate in the larger communities themselves.[3]

PROFIT OR MARKET SHARE?

In looking at the way a large corporation might approach a plant location search from start to final location selection, Robert D. Dean and Thomas M. Carroll (both with the Department of Economics at Memphis State University) analyzed the decision-making process of a large multinational they call XYZ Corporation.[4]

XYZ has two major operating objectives which it ties

directly to plant location decisions: profit and market share. Based on past experience, XYZ has developed target rates of return of the different types of plants it operates. Thus, the estimated rate of return from alternative locations can be compared against an average rate of return from existing plants. In other words, when competition is not a factor, emphasis centers on finding the least-cost plant sites and making certain that conditions that might negatively affect pricing, output, or marketing strategies are minimized.

When rivals are already in the chosen market region, or likely to be, the site search is less intensive and more effort is spent on developing a marketing program that will secure a "fair share" for the plant's products.

XYZ has developed a very thorough procedure for evaluating a subregion. For example, a tax specialist reviews all state tax programs (present and likely) and determines their possible impact on the proposed plant's operating costs, prices, and output. The specialist then ranks the states on those same three factors.

XYZ likes to start with 80 to 100 communities and then narrow that list to about 15, keeping in mind that the community must be capable of absorbing the new plant. Next, the search team develops a five-year production cost schedule for the proposed plant and measures the impact of the new plant's production schedule on the area's public and private resources. This would take into consideration whether any changes would be required in the access routes to the plant, the availability of water and gas supplies, and the community's possible reaction to traffic congestion and pollution. Also, the team would project the payroll's impact on the local wage structure and whether XYZ might have to pay an increasingly larger share of local taxes.

The search team then presents its findings to the planning

153

division of XYZ, including the team's opinion as to whether the local public officials would respond favorably to the company's needs as they develop. The three communities with the highest combined ratings on cost and control are submitted to the executive level for final review. Negotiations then open with the top-ranked community. If satisfactory progress has not been made within a specified length of time, efforts switch to the next choice.

The company searching for a place to locate an office building or plant has basically two choices: (1) a single tract of land upon which it can build one or more facilities or (2) a portion of a larger tract of land which includes numerous sites developed for a similar purpose (an industrial or office park) or for mixed use (a Planned Unit Development, or PUD).

According to *Site Selection Handbook*, the number of planned parks had grown from some 1250 in 1965 to about 4000 by 1977. It defines an industrial park as "a tract of 25 acres or more, under the control and ownership of a single body, with permitted uses regulated by protective covenants."[5] (For office parks, the publication does not set a size limitation.)

Every November the magazine publishes a listing of the available parks within each state along with the latest quoted price per acre and other useful details . Two reasons a company might choose an industrial or office park over a single site, suggests the magazine, are:

1. It provides a means of avoiding much of the governmental bureaucracy that can accompany a move, including Environmental Impact Reports. An industrial park will have already obtained its environmental approvals and permits, built a road system, and installed utilities.

2. Most industrial parks have proved themselves capable of self-policing via deed covenants and performance standards (Figure 16).

While industrial parks provide for many companies the protection they seek for their investment, others prefer the controlled environment or prestige that a single site can offer. The appearance of an industrial park depends upon both the neighbors and the developer doing their part, while the single site offers total control.

TAXES

The projected outlays for state and local taxes can determine location when other factors for rival sites are equal. Table 17 compares the various states. The corporate income tax is the most significant.

An analysis of nine metropolitan counties in northern New Jersey found that industry does respond to variations in local property taxes and that the response is not related to any specific group of "tax-sensitive" industries.[6] A 1958–1967 case study of forty-three Connecticut cities and towns came to the same conclusion.[7] The latter study also found both large and small manufacturing firms sensitive. And a comparison of city-suburb tax differentials noted that the negative impact of a municipal income tax appears greater than that of the local property tax.[8]

Thus, attractive communities with relatively low tax rates may experience net gains in industrial activity.[9] Conversely, less growth or even shrinkage might be expected for cities and towns with relatively high tax rates.

The location decision maker should compare the tax rate of the target area with that of the adjoining communities. If

FIG. 16   Uniform outline for deed covenants and performance standards. (SOURCE: *Site Selection Handbook*, 1977, p. 345. Reproduced by permission of Conway Publications, Inc., Atlanta, Georgia.)

I. Introductory section
   1. Purpose
   2. Ownership
   3. Property description and location
   4. Definitions
II. Land-use criteria
   1. Allowable land-use
   2. Prohibited land-use
   3. Special uses
III. Performance Standards (except local, state, federal, environmental regulations).
   1. Noise
   2. Fire and explosives
   3. Vibration or shock
   4. Smoke or heat
   5. Illumination or glare
   6. Particulate matter, dust and dirt
   7. Electrical disturbances
   8. Odors, toxic or noxious matter
   9. Drainage
   10. Excavation
   11. Radiation
IV. Space allocations and dimensional standards
   1. Building-to-land ratio
      Minimum building size
      Minimum lot size

   2. Setbacks - front yard
   3. Setbacks - side yard
   4. Setbacks - rear yard
   5. Exceptions to side yard and rear yard limits
   6. Rail siding
   7. Height limitations
      Allowable variations
   8. Off-street parking areas
   9. Off-street loading areas
   10. Easements and rights-of-way
   11. Streets and driveways
   12. Sidewalks and curbing
V. Architectural and Aesthetic Standards
   1. Landscaping and limitations on cutting natural growth
   2. Exterior construction, permitted materials, prohibited materials, approved construction methods
   3. Signs
   4. Outdoor storage
   5. Maintenance requirements, refuse collection and prohibition of junk storage

FIG. 16 (*Continued*)

---

6. Utilities placement and design

VI. Implementation of Plans and Construction
1. Architectural review and approval of building plans—procedure
2. Extension to include additional property
3. Developers right to alter or change covenants
4. Enforcement
5. Fees

6. Property owners association
7. Repurchase rights
8. Separability
9. Termination and modifications
10. Constructive notice and acceptance
11. Completion of construction, temporary structures
12. Miscellaneous

VII Special provisions peculiar to project or site

Reasonable deed covenants and performance standards will continue to enjoy high acceptance among facilities planners because they protect a company's investment in an industrial park. To make the process of compliance with standards easier, the Industrial Development Research Council has created a uniform outline for deed covenants and performance standards to allow facilities planners to make comparisons among restrictions at different industrial parks. The outline does not promote specific standards, but rather organizes the various restrictions into a uniform format so that provisions may be compared.

---

it is higher, then caution is in order to make sure that your company will not be called upon to bear a higher and higher share of the future tax burden.

Depending upon the type of company, several other taxes might be of importance. Among them: use taxes on equipment and materials; personal property taxes on inventories; utility connection, or use tax; unemployment insurance;

TABLE 17 State-by-State Comparison of Corporate Income, Sales, Vehicle Fuel, Franchise, and Severance Taxes

	Franchise tax	Corporate income tax (percent)	Federal income tax deductibility	Vehicle fuel tax*a (¢/gal)	Severance tax Oil	Oil	Coal	Other	Sales tax b (percent)
Alabama	$3/1,000 capital stock	5%	Yes	7¢–8¢	2%	2%	13.5¢/ton	Yes	4%
Alaska	—	5.4% + 4% surcharge	No	8	12.25% or 80¢/bbl	10% or 6.4¢/Mcf.	7%	Yes	—
Arizona	—	10.5	Yes	8	—	—	—	—	4
Arkansas	0.11% of outstanding stock	6	No	8.5–9.5	5%	3 mills/Mcf.	2¢/ton	Yes	3c
California	—	9	No	7	Variable 5%+1 mill/$1	Variable 5%+1 mill/$1	—	—	6
Colorado	$10–250	5	No	7	—	—	60¢/ton	Yes	3
Connecticut	—	10	No	11	—	—	—	—	7
Delaware	$60.50/10,000 shares + 30.25 for each added 10,000 shares	7.2	No	11	—	—	—	—	—
Florida	—	5	No	8	8%	5%	5%	Yes	4
Georgia	$5,000 over $22 million	6	No	7.5	—	—	—	—	3
Hawaii	—	6.435	No	8.5	—	—	—	—	0.5c
Idaho	$300 over $2 million	6.5	No	9.5	5 mills/bbl max.	5 mills/Mcf. max.	2%	Yes	3

Illinois	0.1% of stated capital	4	No	7.5	—	—	—	—	4
Indiana	—	3	No	8	1%	—	—	—	4
Iowa	$5–3,000	10	Yes	7–8	—	—	—	—	3c
Kansas	$20–2,5000	2.25	No	8	4.5 mills/bbl	8.06 mills/Mcf.	—	—	3c
Kentucky	70¢/$1,000	5.8	No	9	0.5–1.5%	—	4.5% or 50¢/ton 10¢/ton	—	5
Louisiana	$1.50/$1,000 of capital stock	8	Yes	8	12.5%	7¢/Mcf.	—	—	3
Maine	—	6.93	No	9	—	—	—	—	5
Maryland	—	7	No	9	—	—	—	—	5
Massachusetts	$5.76/$1,000 tangible property	8.33%d	No	8.5	—	—	—	—	5
Michigan	—	2.35j	—	9–7	2%	2%	—	—	4
Minnesota	—	12	Yes	9	—	—	—	Yes	4
Mississippi	$2.50/$1,000	4	No	9–10	6% or 6¢/bbl	6% or 3 mills/Mcf.	—	Yes	5c
Missouri	0.05% par value of outstanding stock and surplus	5	Yes	7	—	—	—	—	3.125
Montana	—	6.75	No	8–10	2.65% + 0.2¢/bbl	2.65% + 0.2¢/10 Mcf	12¢—40¢/ton. or 4%–30%	Yes	—

TABLE 17 (Continued)

	Franchise tax	Corporate income tax (percent)	Federal income tax deductibility	Vehicle "fuel tax*" (¢/gal.)	Severance tax				Sales tax (percent)
					Oil	Oil	Coal	Other	
Nebraska	$10–8,250	4.4	No	9.5(4.5)^e	—	—	—	—	3
Nevada	—	—	—	6	—	—	—	—	3
New Hampshire	$60–2,000	5	No	10	—	—	—	—	—
New Jersey	2mills/$1 for $100 million + 0.2–0.4 mill/$1 for over $100 million	7.25	No	8	—	—	—	—	5
New Mexico	55¢/$1,000	5 or 0.75^c	No	7	3.75% + privilege tax	3.75% + privilege tax	0.5%	Yes	4
New York	Alternatives in lieu of income tax	10	No	8–10	—	—	—	—	4
North Carolina	$1.50/$1,000	6	No	9	—	—	—	—	3
North Dakota	—	6	Yes	8	5%	5%	65¢/ton^f	—	3^c
Ohio	8%*	—	—	7	3¢/bbl	1¢/Mcf.	4¢/ton	Yes	4
Oklahoma	$10–20,000	4	No	6.58	7% + 0.085%/ bbl	7% + 0.085%/ Mcf.	—	Yes	2
Oregon	$200	7.5	No	7	—	—	—	Yes	—
Pennsylvania	10 mills/ taxable $1	10.5	No	9	—	—	—	—	6
Rhode Island	—	8	No	10	—	—	—	—	6

160

South Carolina	1 mill/$1	6	No	9	—	—	—	—	4
South Dakota	—	5.5	Yes	8	—	—	—	—	4
Tennessee	15¢/$100	6	No	7	—	—	—	—	3[h]
Texas	$4.25/$1,000	—	—	5–6.5	4.6%+ 3/16¢/bbl	7.5%	—	Yes	4
Utah	—	4	Yes	9	2%+2 mills/$1	2%+2 mills/$1	—	Yes	4
Vermont	—	7.5	No	9	—	—	—	—	3
Virginia	$20–20,000	6	No	9	—	—	—	Yes	3
Washington	$30–2,500	—	—	11	—	—	—	—	4.6[i]
West Virginia	$20/2,500	6	No	10.5	—	—	—	—	3
Wisconsin	—	7.9	10% of net income	7	—	—	—	—	4
Wyoming	$50/$1 million	—	—	8	2%+0.3 mill/$1	2%+0.3 mill/$1	8.5%	Yes	3

a. Where taxes on gasoline and diesel fuel differ, both are shown, with gasoline tax first.

b. Sales tax data apply to statewide levies only; in some states, communities impose local sales taxes. Corporate income tax shown is maximum rate applicable; most states have sliding scales with lower tax on small businesses.

c. Gross receipts.

d. Massachusetts: plus 14% surcharge, and $2.60/$1,000 (plus 14% surcharge) property tax.

e. Nebraska: gasoline blend with 10% (99%) ethanol.

f. North Dakota: from July 1, 1977, through June 30, 1979.

g. Ohio: or 5 mills/$1 of issue and outstanding shares, whichever is greater.

h. Tennessee: rate was 4.5 from April 1, 1976, through June 30, 1978.

i. Washington: from June 1, 1976, through June 30, 1979.

j. Michigan: has single, unique tax related to profits earned, interest paid compensation paid and depreciation.

SOURCE: Commerce Clearing House.

workmen's compensation charges; fuel taxes; and school and other special taxes.

CHOOSING A DEVELOPER

Now that you've chosen the community, how do you go about evaluating the developer? James Rouse, Chairman of the Board of the Rouse Company and the entrepreneur who conceived the Columbia, Maryland, new-town concept, offers these suggestions:

> First, look at the developer's experience record. What has he done before? Was it quality work—aesthetically pleasing, with an attractive entrance, good landscaping, well-designed and constructed roads, adequate parking, and the total package appropriate to the intended use?
> Next, consider the reputation of the developer and his financial capability to do what's supposed to be done. The performance record can be checked by talking with those who manage the businesses in his developments and with officials of the local government and local bankers. And the shorter the amount of time the developer has been in business the more you should examine his available financial reserves.
> Finally, consider the developer's organization. Who does he have to work with you? Is it a one man show or does he have a real development team? Generally speaking, the better developers have sales, engineering and maintenance personnel.
> Putting it another way, the risk decreases directly with the experience of the developer, his reputation, financial strength and organizational capabilities to carry out the project. If you go with someone who has less than that to offer (and there are some good individual or small developers),

then *you* had better have the organization yourself to oversee the venture to completion.

OWN OR LEASE?

Having selected a location and a site, the last question becomes whether to own or lease. Each has advantages.

Ownership means a lower annual cost of occupancy. The interest on the mortgage plus the maintenance and depreciation costs can be deducted from corporate income taxes. You are assured of permanence of address, can lease space to other tenants for additional income, and have real prop-

---

FIG. 17 Site selection checklist. (SOURCE: *Factory Management and Maintenance*, May 1957, pp. 180+.) Reprinted by permission of Morgan Gampian Company.

---

31. Specific Site Considerations	*Importance*	*Site*
Is your product such that advertising value plays a big part in site selection as well as plant appearance?	☐	☐
Has character of site been thoroughly explored? Typical factors:	☐	☐
a. Topography.		
b. Size of area available for purchase.		
c. Layout and orientation.		
d. Drainage.		
e. Freedom from flooding.		
f. Any utilities already in place?		
g. Subsoil, excavation, and foundation considerations.		
h. Gullies, streams, etc., to be bridged.		

FIG. 17 (*Continued*)

	Importance	*Site*
i. Any abnormal grading or landscaping problems?		
j. Any pipelines or other utilities to be relocated?		
Are general construction costs competitive with those of competing sites?	☐	☐
Is site convenient for noon-hour shopping?	☐	☐
If in limestone country, any tell-tale sinkholes?	☐	☐
Is site near enough an airport that CAB regulations must be considered in making building plans?	☐	☐
Any restrictive covenants, easements, or other legal entanglements that would interfere with use of property?	☐	☐

32. Police Aspects

Does police department have high standards of personnel, equipment, training, morale?	☐	☐
Is police patrol service provided for industrial properties?	☐	☐
Are there satisfactory policing arrangements outside city limits?	☐	☐
Are private watchmen services or uniformed detective agencies available?	☐	☐
Is incidence of crime as low as or lower than in surrounding area?	☐	☐
Does community have a disproportionate number of bars and taverns?	☐	☐
Is judiciary system well organized?	☐	☐

33. Fire Aspects

Does fire department have high standards of personnel, equipment, training, morale?	☐	☐

	Importance	*Site*
Are community fire insurance classifications up near the top?	☐	☐
In case of serious fire, are adjacent communities near enough to send apparatus?	☐	☐
Is site within fire hydrant limits?	☐	☐
If so, are mains sized adequately?	☐	☐
Are water pressure and reserve capacity sufficient for your needs?	☐	☐

34. Roads and Highways

Does quality of construction and maintenance indicate an efficient highway department?	☐	☐
Does local highway system have adequate interconnections with national network?	☐	☐
Are roads kept free of ice and snow?	☐	☐
Is there a well-planned highway improvement program?	☐	☐
Is proportion of unimproved roads steadily being reduced?	☐	☐

35. Trash and Garbage

Is potential site within pickup limits?	☐	☐
If not, are private contractors available?	☐	☐
Does Board of Health exercise supervisory inspections over garbage collection methods?	☐	☐

36. Sewage

Is site within sewage system limits?	☐	☐
Can system handle your requirements?	☐	☐
Does sewage department have realistic plans for expanding its network and equipment?	☐	☐

erty that can serve as security for a loan or be sold with a possible capital profit.

Leasing offers a fixed and known cost of occupancy with the rent deductible from income taxes. No capital is tied up in land, bricks or mortar but the lease can be sold as a part of the business. The period of commitment and extent of liability are limited.

Finally, lease decisions require less advance planning. Both owning and leasing, however, require the counsel of a real estate consultant, a lawyer, and an income tax adviser.[10]

NOTES

1. Kennith H. Ripnen, *Office Space Administration*, (revised 2d ed. of *Office Building and Office Layout Planning*), McGraw-Hill, 1974.

2. Prentice L. Knight, III, *Intraurban Industrial Location Factors from the Viewpoint of Manufacturing Decision-Makers*, Ph.D. dissertation, University of Illinois at Urbana-Champaign, 1977.

3. Eugene H. Gishlick, *Plant Location in Manufacturing: A Testing of Some Hypotheses*, Ph.D. dissertation, University of Pennsylvania, 1973.

4. Robert D. Dean and Thomas M. Carroll, "Plant Location Under Uncertainty," *Land Economics*, November 1977, pp. 436–444.

5. "More Firms Are Choosing Planned Parks Over Single Sites; SSHB List Pushes 4,000," *Site Selection Handbook*, November 1977, pp. 344–346. (Quoted by permission of Conway Publications, Inc., Atlanta, Georgia.)

6. James E. Frank, *Locational Effects of Local Revenue Systems: The Case of the Property Tax*, Ph.D. dissertation, New York University, 1971.

7. Robert Farrington, *Local Property Tax Rates and Intraregional Plant Location: A Case Study in Connecticut 1958–1967*, Ph.D. dissertation, Fordham University, 1975.

8. Roger W. Schmenner, *City Taxes and Industry Location*, Ph.D. dissertation, Yale University, 1973.

9. Robert Farrington, op. cit.

10. David Scribner, "How to Find the Best Location for Your Business," Section 6, *J. K. Lasser's Business Management Handbook*, 3rd ed., Bernard Greisman, ed., 1968, pp. 203–204.

ELEVEN

Handling
Individual Transfers

Each year an estimated 40 million Americans change their home address. About 12 million of these move across state and county lines. Though most moves are made voluntarily, probably around 800,000 men, women, and children change their address at an employer's behest—some 200,000 to 300,000 corporate transfers annually.

"The most frequent cause is a manpower need at a particular location; for example, a manager is required at a branch where qualified personnel are not already available," explains William F. Glueck, a management specialist and faculty member at the University of Missouri-Columbia. "A second reason for managerial transfer is to fulfill plans for the career development of executives. Some firms, usually large national companies with diversity in the product/service offering, have devised plans that involve cross-functional and geographic transfers as part of managerial development. In these instances, transfers are probably essential. A third case of managerial transfer is the physical relocation of facilities."[1]

Ernest L. Hoffman, Jr., assistant vice president for employee relations of the State Farm Mutual Automobile Insurance Company, says that his firm has identified three categories of problems that are particularly critical when management decides to relocate an employee.

The first, external conditions, are those beyond the control of the company: for example, a depressed real estate market in one area or an inflated market in another. Employees in such situations may turn down or be bypassed for a transfer even if it includes a promotion simply because of the financial hardship the move would create.

A second factor that comes into play is the transferee's expectations. A 1977 survey of 167 State Farm employees found that the average selling price of their homes was $43,259 while the purchase price averaged $54,597—a 26 percent upgrading. Likewise, the old home averaged 1627 square feet but the new one averaged 1835 feet—an increase of roughly 13 percent. "Based on these statistics," states Hoffman, "we concluded that the employee feels that 'buying up' is expected and that the company will assist him in his real estate improvement."

As troublesome as such expectations can be for the routine transfer, "it can be an even greater problem with executive relocations," notes Hoffman. An executive who experiences a bad move can create a negative attitude in the company toward the relocation program and produce a long-lasting problem. Observes Hoffman: "For this reason, we consider executive relocations to be a very special high-priority interest of everyone responsible for administering our program."

The third category of relocation problems is communication. This can include misunderstandings about what the company's relocation program will or will not do, poor communications between the representative of the relocation company (if one is hired) and the employee, bad impressions left by the company appraiser—perhaps by too casual an attitude—and by an unrealistic market price quoted by real estate brokers in order to obtain the right to sell the employee's home.[2]

SELLING THE OLD HOUSE

The most important changes in relocation policies have to do with selling and buying houses. More and more companies are hastening the executive's move by assurance of a buyer, for his or her home, usually a relocation service such as Merrill Lynch Relocation Management, Homequity/ Homerica, Executrans, or the Equitable Relocation Service.

"The sale of the employee's existing home is not only the most expensive part of the transfer but also the most sensitive one," points out George H. Rathman, president of Merrill Lynch Relocation Management Inc. "For many employees, their home represents their most significant investment and obtaining the highest possible price is an important objective."[3] Merrill Lynch has broken the sale of the old home into five major cost areas (Figure 18). The Tax Grossup entry in Figure 18 covers the additional tax liability the employee may incur (the Internal Revenue Service now treats part of the company's payment to the employee as earned income).

The cost of employee travel and temporary living expenses, estimated to average $2,300 in 1977, results in part, according to Rathman, "because companies often give their employees short notice when they ask them to accept a new position. The employee may move several weeks or

FIG. 18 1977 relocation costs for typical transfer. (SOURCE: George H. Rathman, "Lowering the High Cost of Moving," *Proceedings of Relocation Management '78*, Merrill Lynch Relocation Management Inc., 1979, p. 17.)

Employee travel and temporary living		$ 2,300
Family travel and shipment of household goods		4,500
Sale of old home:		
Duplicate housing	1,400	
Loss on sale below fair market value	700	
Brokerage commission	3,300	
Other closing costs	800	
Cost of equity advances	500	
		6,700
Purchase of and resettling in new home		700
Tax gross-up		1,800
Total costs		$16,000

even months before the rest of the family, leaving the spouse and children behind to sell the existing home and arrange for the move."

A survey of 600 leading corporations by Merrill Lynch found that the percentage of companies protecting their employees against any loss below market value for their homes has been increasing sharply, rising from 27 percent in 1973 to 45 percent in 1976. What's more, the number of companies employing the services of an outside location firm climbed from 19 percent in 1973 to 34 percent in 1976. Table 18 outlines the various forms this can take. Table 19 presents the same data categorized by the number of home-owners transferred by the company.

As Table 19 shows, 82 percent of the companies surveyed that transfer 500 or more employees either buy the trans-feree's home through a company "purchase plan" or retain a relocation firm to buy it, while only 18 percent are involved in some kind of reimbursement plan. The same kind of dis-tinction exists by industry. The energy companies—oil and

TABLE 18 Policy With Respect to Disposing of Former Residency by Year

	1976 % using	1973 % using	(1973–1976) % change
The company employs an outside firm	34%	19%	15%
The company offers to purchase the employee's home	11%	8%	3%
The employee must arrange for the sale but is reimbursed for some or all expenses	46%	53%	− 7%
The employee is not given any assistance or reimbursement in the sale of home	7%	14%	− 7%
Other Policies	2%	6%	− 4%
	100%	100%	

SOURCE: Weston E. Edwards, "Prescriptions for Relocation Policy—Coping with the Forces of Change," *Proceedings of Relocation Management '78*, Merrill Lynch Relocation Management Inc., p. 51.

TABLE 19   Policy with Respect to Disposing of Former Residence by Transfer Volume

	No. of transferred homeowners:					
	Under 25	25–49	50–99	100–249	250–499	500 or more
Company employs an outside firm	21%	37%	41%	40%	53%	73%
Company offers to purchase the employee's home	9%	12%	9%	15%	19%	9%
Employee must arrange for the sale but is reimbursed for some or all expenses	56%	47%	44%	43%	28%	18%
Employee is not given assistance or reimbursement	14%	4%	6%	2%	—	—

SOURCE: Weston E. Edwards, "Prescriptions for Relocation Policy—Coping with the Forces of Change," *Proceedings of Relocation Management '78*, Merrill Lynch Relocation Management Inc., p. 52.

gas—are heavily involved in providing comprehensive assistance, while the retailing and wholesaling companies have been slow in responding to this trend.

What relocation services do to justify their fee is speed the move for the employee's family by purchasing the employee's home, expedite the shipping of household goods, free the company of the administrative chores related to such moves, and reduce the amount of tax gross-up a company pays the employee. And since the relocation service buys the house (for the company), one of the largest "income" items—the brokerage commission—can be eliminated.

Although the law could change, observes Merrill Lynch's Rathman, the most recent rulings "make it clear that under either an in-house or third party purchase program, none of the expenses incurred by the employer or by the service firm constitute wages or compensation of any sort to the transferee. Also, these expenses and payments should be recognized as ordinary and necessary business expenses to the employer, deductible in full as paid or accrued by the employer."

BUYING THE NEW HOUSE

Figures from the National Association of Realtors indicate that while housing costs are stabilizing in the Northeast, they are still escalating at a rapid clip elsewhere (Table 20).

The problem this presents for the transferee can be seen from Tables 21 and 22. As these tables indicate, in 1968, 82 percent of the existing homes and 71 percent of the newly constructed homes in the United States were priced under $30,000; now only 25 percent of existing homes and 7 percent of new homes cost under $30,000. On the other hand, in 1968 only 6 percent of all homes sold for more than $50,-000. Now 38 percent of existing homes and 47 percent of new homes fall into that category.

A comparison of interest rates (Table 23) provides another indication of the rising cost of home ownership. The situa-

TABLE 20 Percent Change of Housing Costs by Region

	Increase mid-1976–1977	Increase mid-1977–1978
United States	12.4%	11.5%
Northeast	7.9%	2.7%
North Central	10.4%	14.5%
South	8.0%	11.4%
West	26.9%	13.4%

SOURCE: National Association of Realtors.

175

TABLE 21 Price Range of Existing Houses—1968–1977
Totals may not equal 100% due to rounding

Year	Under $30,000	$30,000–39,999	$40,000–49,999	Over $50,000
1968	82%	11%	14%	3%
69	76	14	5	4
70	73	16	6	5
71	67	18	8	7
72	61	20	10	9
73	53	22	12	13
74	45	24	14	17
75	37	24	16	22
76	32	23	18	28
77	25	20	17	38

SOURCE: National Association of Realtors.

TABLE 22 Price Range of New Houses—1968–1977
Totals may not equal 100% due to rounding

Year	Under $30,000	$30,000–39,999	$40,000–49,999	Over $50,000
1968	71%	21%	6%	3%
69	66	22	8	4
70	73	17	8	4
71	66	20	8	6
72	59	24	10	7
73	41	31	15	12
74	28	35	19	17
75	21	32	23	24
76	12	26	26	35
77	7	21	24	47

SOURCE: U.S. League of Savings Associations.

tion presents a serious financial burden for many transferees, particularly those moving from a rural to an urban area.

Policies toward the reimbursement of home purchase expenses have also been changing, points out the chairman

TABLE 23   Terms on Conventional Mortgage
Loans

Year	Newly built homes		Previously occupied homes	
	Effective rate %	Purchase price ($000)	Effective rate %	Purchase price ($000)
Dec. 1973	8.49	38.3	8.74	29.7
Dec. 1974	9.31	43.0	9.75	34.8
Dec. 1975	9.05	46.1	9.34	37.2
Dec. 1976	9.12	50.0	9.14	43.0
Dec. 1977	9.13	58.0	9.18	48.9
July 1978	9.59	60.1	9.72	51.0

SOURCE: United States League of Saving Associations, *Savings and Loan '78 Fact Book*.

and chief executive officer of Merrill Lynch Relocation Management Inc., Dr. Weston E. Edwards. As shown in Table 24, companies have been increasing the level of benefits extended. "The last item on the chart, mortagage rate differential," points out Dr. Edwards, "is a new area some companies are experimenting with. The number testing this benefit has increased from a mere 7 percent in 1973 to 11 percent in 1976. Also, the percentage of firms 'grossing up,' as it is called, to offset the additional tax liability caused by relocation reimbursements, rose from 38 percent in 1972 to 62 percent in 1976."[4]

H. Cris Collie, executive director of the Employee Relocation Council (ERC), informs us that 105 of ERC's 600 member companies now provide some form of direct assistance if the executive's new mortgage interest rate is higher than the old one. This is double the number that paid this benefit four years ago, notes Collie.

Statistics based on responses from 310 of ERC's member

TABLE 24   Reimbursement of Home Purchase Expenses
% of firms who reimbursed

	In 1976	In 1975	In 1974	In 1973	% change 1973–1976
All normal closing costs	57%	56%	52%	48%	+ 9%
Attorney or escrow fees	56%	55%	49%	46%	+10%
Title costs	55%	53%	50%	46%	+ 9%
Mortgage origination fees	45%	43%	35%	34%	+11%
Mortgage discount points	31%	33%	29%	25%	+ 6%
Interest on interim or bridge loans	30%	27%	19%	23%	+ 7%
Mortgage rate differential between old and new homes	11%	13%	8%	7%	+ 4%

SOURCE: Weston E. Edwards, "Prescriptions for Relocation Policy—Coping with the Forces of Change," *Proceedings of Relocation Management '78*, Merrill Lynch Relocation Management Inc., p. 51.

companies reveal that the average cost of relocating a homeowner in 1978 was $12,787, up 9.0 percent from the 1977 average of $11,739 and more than 64 percent from the average cost in 1973 of $7,800. These costs reflect not only the sharply escalating home prices that generate higher broker commissions on the old house but also increased relocation benefits at the new location. The average cost of relocating a renter in 1978 was $4,271, says ERC, up 7.0 percent from the 1977 average of $3,980.

The typical ERC member company transfers 160 homeowners, 80 renters, and 83 new hires each year. "At the 1978 average costs," notes Collie, "the average total relocation expense budget for this typical ERC member exceeds $2.5 million annually. The survey also found that 93 percent of the nondiscretionary costs of a transferee's expenses are covered by the typical Employee Relocation Council member company. Also, only 10 percent of the 310 respondents indicated they were encountering difficulty in getting employees to accept transfers. However, 35 percent indicated that the high cost of housing in such states as California, New York and New Jersey created problems in persuading employees to move to certain cities."

CHECKLISTS OF BENEFITS

As adapted from Employee Relocation Council material, here are the costs which an employee is likely to encounter and which could be covered by a company program:

1. *Present Housing.* Brokerage fees and other expenses incidental to sale such as mortgage prepayment penalty and closing costs. Any loss incurred because of the sale. For renters, lease cancellation fees or rental for balance of lease period if unable to sublet.

2. *Househunting trips.* All expenses for transferee and spouse to the new location to seek housing.

3. *Employee Return Trips.* Travel and related expenses between old and new location if employee begins new job and has to leave family behind.

4. *Down Payment Requirement.* Companies may provide a bridge loan, often interest-free, when the employee's old home remains unsold and a down payment is required on the new home.

5. *Closing Costs on New House.* Mortgage-related expenses at the new location.

6. *Moving of Furniture and Personal Belongings.* Includes packing, insuring, and storing, when necessary.

179

7. *Travel to New Location*. Transfer costs for employee and family, including meals, motels, and incidentals.
8. *Miscellaneous Expenses*. Temporary living costs at old or new location, costs of cleaning and recutting drapes and rugs, etc.

NEW HIRES

While the corporate relocation policies for current employees are generally well defined and, for the most part quite generous, those for the new hire generally offer "bare bones" coverage and any additional coverage depends a great deal on the level and insistence of the new employee.

The Employee Relocation Council surveyed its member companies in 1977 on their current relocation practices with new hires. A portion of the results appear in Table 25.

On the executive level, nearly all moving-related expenses are paid for in full or in part, or can be negotiated as a condition of hire. Items the executives have the least chance of obtaining are equity loans and miscellaneous allowances. And some 20 percent of companies never offer the newly hired executive any reimbursement for real estate sales expenses or lease-breaking penalties. As for anything extra for any tax-accrued liabilities, the chances are 3 to 1 that the executive won't collect.[5]

Experienced middle management (and highly specialized or technical employees) fare about as well as executives on their reimbursement for basic temporary living costs. For everything else, however, the chances of negotiating additional coverage are about 1 in 3. If it is not the policy of a company to cover real estate sales expenses for such new hires but where the potential employee insists, explains ERC's Collie, "the personnel manager may go to the man-

TABLE 25 The Expenses Reimbursements Made to Various Types of New Hires

	Recent college graduates		Experienced middle management		Executive level	
	No. of co.	% of total	No. of co.	% of total	No. of co.	% of total
Temporary living expenses						
Covered by policy, *full reimbursement*	146	57.5%	175	68.1%	172	69.6%
Covered by policy, *partial reimbursement*	34	13.4%	25	9.7%	21	8.5%
Not covered by policy, *usually negotiable*	10	3.9%	17	6.6%	20	8.1%
Not covered by policy, *sometimes negotiable*	24	9.4%	22	8.6%	16	6.5%
Not covered by policy, *never negotiable*	22	8.7%	4	1.5%	2	0.8%
Level of assistance not specified/no answer	13	5.1%	11	4.3%	12	4.8%
Real estate–sales expenses						
Covered by policy, *full reimbursement*	5	2.0%	35	13.5%	51	20.7%
Covered by policy, *partial reimbursement*	3	1.2%	11	4.3%	9	3.6%
Not covered by policy, *usually negotiable*	4	1.6%	20	7.8%	55	22.3%
Not covered by policy, *sometimes negotiable*	32	12.6%	64	24.9%	61	24.7%
Not covered by policy, *never negotiable*	177	69.7%	101	39.5%	49	19.8%
Level of assistance not specified/no answer	28	11.0%	23	9.0%	18	7.3%
Equity loans						
Covered by policy, *full reimbursement*	11	4.3%	32	12.5%	42	17.0%
Covered by policy, *partial reimbursement*	3	1.2%	4	1.6%	4	1.6%
Not covered by policy, *usually negotiable*	4	1.6%	10	3.9%	29	11.7%
Not covered by policy, *sometimes negotiable*	15	5.9%	49	19.1%	52	21.0%
Not covered by policy, *never negotiable*	188	74.0%	136	52.9%	96	38.9%
Level of assistance not specified/no answer	26	2.4%	23	9.0%	20	8.1%
Tax liability						
Covered by policy, *full reimbursement*	84	33.1%	92	35.8%	97	39.3%
Covered by policy, *partial reimbursement*	25	9.9%	28	10.9%	27	10.9%
Not covered by policy, *usually negotiable*	2	0.8%	9	3.5%	17	6.9%
Not covered by policy, *sometimes negotiable*	13	5.1%	19	7.4%	26	10.5%
Not covered by policy, *never negotiable*	101	39.8%	88	34.2%	62	25.1%
Level of assistance not specified/no answer	24	9.5%	18	7.0%	14	6.5%
Miscellaneous allowance						
Covered by policy, *full reimbursement*	26	10.2%	49	19.1%	55	22.3%
Covered by policy, *partial reimbursement*	22	8.7%	24	9.3%	22	8.9%
Not covered by policy, *usually negotiable*	6	2.4%	11	4.3%	20	8.1%
Not covered by policy, *sometimes negotiable*	24	9.4%	27	10.5%	37	15.0%
Not covered by policy, *never negotiable*	139	54.7%	117	45.5%	85	34.4%
Level of assistance not specified	32	12.6%	26	10.2%	24	9.7%

SOURCE: *Mini-Survey of New Hires and Group Moves*, Employee Relocation Council, pp. 4–7.

ager involved in making the hire and ask . . . if it's worth say $3,000 from his or her budget to have this particular candidate. Real estate sales assistance is the most expensive aspect of any relocation program. It is not surprising, therefore, that few recent college graduates are covered under a company's policy, while executive new hires have a better chance of coverage, and middle management and the highly specialized-technical employees slightly less chance than the executive level yet stand a much better probability of having their real estate expenses covered than the fresh graduate."

NOTES

1. William F. Glueck, "Managers, Mobility, and Morale," *Business Horizons*, December 1974, pp. 65–70.
2. Ernest L. Hoffman, Jr., "A Little Talk Goes a Long Way," *Proceedings of Relocation Management '78*, Merrill Lynch Relocation Management, Inc., 1978, pp. 33–39.
3. George H. Rathman, "Lowering the High Cost of Moving," *Proceedings of Relocation Management '78*, Merrill Lynch Relocation Management Inc., 1978, pp. 15–24.
4. Weston E. Edwards, "Prescriptions for Relocation Policy: Coping with the Forces of Change," *Proceedings of Relocation Management '78*, Merrill Lynch Relocation Management Inc., 1978, pp. 51–65.
5. *Mini-Survey of New Hires and Group Moves*, Employee Relocation Council, August 1977.

TWELVE

Coordinating
Group Moves

Group moves present a special set of problems. The careful planning and management of group moves is as important as the decision to move. Just using the existing policy for mass moves is probably not the best approach to take.

While individual transfers generally entail salary increases and/or promotions, these moves don't. And group moves frequently deal with people who have lived in one place all of their lives, so the problems are different. They must break longstanding family and social ties. You have to be prepared to answer the question: Why am I moving; what is in it for me? Why is the company moving? What is the company going to do for me?

The first step might be formation of a relocation committee of about six key people to develop a policy for the move. Another step would be a questionnaire to all employees to find out: whether they are homeowners or renters; mortgage rate; number of children and their schools; and how long they have lived in the area. Realtors from the new area along with representatives from the Chamber of Commerce and the school systems will usually be willing to brief groups on the characteristics of the new area.

Employees can then be asked to commit themselves—yes I will go, no I will not. For those who elect not to go, it makes good sense to offer a bonus and help in finding new employment if they will stay on until the moving date. Those who say yes can be taken on guided tours of the new area and arrangements might even be made for partially subsidized mortgage financing.

Properly handled, a group move can improve morale. One of the real pluses of a group move is that it forces you to establish a new image, to establish a new corporate policy, and to modernize the overall existing policies.

GROUP MOVE STATISTICS

Of the 277 companies that participated in the Employee Relocation Council's (ERC) survey, "New Hires and Group Moves," 103 reported experience with a mass move between 1972 and 1977.[1] Of these companies, 22 (21.4 percent) had two such moves and 26 (25.2 percent) had three or more.

While a group move by definition usually refers to one of 20 or more employees, those covered by the ERC survey ranged from 6 to 2000, with an average of 162 employees being requested to transfer. Of those offered a move, about 75 percent accepted, although the acceptance rate ranged from 18 percent to 100 percent. One company with a low "acceptance rate" pointed out that 90 percent of its exempt employees agreed to the transfer, while only 25 percent of the nonexempt personnel were willing to move.

For exempt personnel, companies were about evenly divided on whether to use the regular relocation policy or to devise a special one. For companies who made two or more moves over the five-year span of the survey, about 70 percent had a regular relocation policy that also served for the group move. Only 25 (24.3 percent) of the 103 companies involved in a group move offered a transfer to nonexempt production personnel. Transfers were offered to about 60 percent of the nonexempt clerical staff and the nonexempt technical staff. In most cases, the nonexempt employee was covered by the regular relocation policy or by a special policy devised for all involved in the mass move. However, 20 percent of the nonexempts were covered only by a special policy applicable to their particular group.

Special provisions for the group move were implemented by many companies. Counseling on both the area and on individual problems was made available by 66 corporations (64.1 percent); normally these were handled by the company, although some employed third-party firms. Special househunting trips to the new location in excess of the regular policy were provided by 53 companies (51.5 percent). And 39 companies (37.9 percent) provided mortgage and other financial assistance, usually through special arrangements with lending institutions. Transfer incentives were offered by 40 companies (38.8 percent). Six such instances involved special automobile financing for employees being transferred out of New York City; in one instance, driver's training courses were provided.

Not all employees requested to move can accept a transfer for various personal reasons. In 78.6 percent (81 companies) of such instances covered by the ERC survey, companies made some form of special provision—severance pay based on years of service, early retirement programs, transfers to other company locations, and/or help in finding a new job.

MANAGING THE MOVE

Many employees may have joined a company because they wanted to stay in their home community and never expected to relocate. "Therefore, greater inducements must be included in a group-move policy to attract the employees you wish to retain and to encourage them to relocate," suggests William S. Gault, vice president of marketing and client relations at Executrans, Inc.[2]

The first step, points out Gault, will be to learn some facts about the employees that are not normally contained in personnel files: How old are the children at home? Do you own your own home, rent, or live with parents? If homeowner, when did you buy? Do you own a car? How do you get to work? Is your spouse employed, and if so, in what type of job? "You will also need to determine how many minority employees are in the group because some will have special problems that need to be individually addressed, rather than covered in the master policy," explains Gault. And the benefits department should determine those employees within five years of normal retirement.

From the questionnaire, a graph of homeowners and renters can be developed to help determine what problems the employees might encounter in finding affordable housing. Also, you should check the local employment market for job possibilities for employees who might decide not to relocate.

"Experience shows that five types of employees are least likely to accept relocation," comments Gault. These are:

1. Young, single, short-service employees
2. Employees with children in high school
3. Employees within five years of normal retirement date
4. Employees with vested interest in the company's retirement plan and whose careers may have topped out
5. Employees whose spouse's career is more important to the family

Careful analysis of the data should enable a company to estimate how many will make the move, retire, or resign so that the proper packages, including severance pay, can be designed and a relocation expense budget set up.

"Whatever your basic approach to relocation," continues Gault, "your specific policy objective should be to: (1) encourage maximum acceptance of the relocation by the desired employees, (2) maintain the highest possible productivity of all employees from the first announcement to the completion of the move, and (3) accomplish the move at minimum dollar cost to the company and minimum psychological cost to each family."

The biggest worry for the relocated family usually is disposing of the present home quickly and at a fair price. The second biggest challenge will be to find a satisfactory home at a price they can afford during a relatively short home-buying trip. This means that you have to know the new area well and provide professional assistance, or employees may make a hasty decision that can adversely affect their future happiness and productivity. "Homesearch trips, however, should not be made to the new area until employees have determined in some reasonable fashion the approximate value of their present homes," points out Gault. They will need this value in order to determine their equity and, consequently, determine the price range of homes they can afford.

MINIMIZING PEOPLE PROBLEMS

"Unless the necessary time and effort are expended by the company, there is a good chance that the primary objective of the group move—to position the relocated business unit and its employees for highest efficiency—will not be attained," states James M. Keane,[3] vice president of client relations and services at Homequity/Homerica. "Mangled moves have been known to precipitate divorces. There also can be delayed effects such as the loss of a valued employee who reluctantly makes the move and eventually loses all motivation and quits."

An important part of the group move is the communication with the employees. A senior executive should send an official announcement to each employee, and group meetings should then be held with employees to explain the business reasons for the move. Each employee should be informed about the relocation assistance policy and what benefits, including severance pay and/or bonus, they will receive if they elect not to move. Then, group meetings should be held in the evenings with families (up to fifty persons) to answer questions and show slides or a film on the new area and to discuss housing, schools, etc.

"Rumors can be devastating to a group move—although they are seldom a problem in an individual move," explains Keane. "Virtually all rumors are created by an absence of information, so the best way to counter them is to be ready with detailed facts."

While the benefits offered may not be much different

from the normal relocation package, companies need to remember that in many cases they are dealing with inexperienced movers. Kean's firm recommends that at least six months be alloted for the move. He notes, "The company that allows a family three to four months to carry through its move will generally find that with proper assistance, virtually all families will actually have been moved in much less time than that. This means that the company has time to adjust its schedules to work most efficiently."

Without proper guidance, the novice mover will rely on a neighbor or relative for advice and possibly make a mistake. That means the company or outside relocation specialists it has hired should be available for coaching and help. The objective is not to make the transferee an expert in home selling, home finding, and moving of household goods, Keane comments, but "it is important to the development of a satisfied transferee that he or she be able to recognize precisely how and why he or she is being treated well. If the employee knows he or she has been handled fairly, top work efficiency will quickly return."

CONSOLIDATION CASE HISTORY

Pulling together the existing operations and people from several plants represents a special problem. Few histories of such moves exist, but that of a particularly complex one was recorded by Edmund S. Whitman and W. James Schmidt in their classic in the field, *Plant Relocation: A Case History of a Move*.

Their company was General Foods Corporation. The situation was the consolidation of four plants of its Jell-O Division into one new facility at Dover, Delaware. Movement of more than 2000 major pieces of equipment was involved.

Approximately 500 employees transferred to the new location or to other General Foods plants, while some 1300 were terminated, elected retirement, or resigned.

Once the decision to consolidate had been made, the employees of the plants affected were informed even before the site had been selected. The company decided to offer a job at the new plant, plus generous moving allowances, to everyone. Over the two years that preceded the first transfers, a series of "On the Move" bulletins were issued under the signature of the division's operations manager. An important factor in assisting employees in moving to the new location was the company's provision for a professional advisor on real estate matters, since many employees were hourly personnel with no experience in disposing of, or acquiring, property.

While the closing of two of the plants (Hoboken, New Jersey, and Dorchester, Massachusetts) would have little impact on the economies of their areas, the Tapioca plant at Orange, Massachusetts, employed 10 percent of that city's employment base, and Jell-O's 370 employees at Le Roy, New York, comprised 25 percent of that city's total employment. In these last two cases, General Foods met the problem head on by meeting with the irate city leaders and offering among other things to underwrite the cost of a community industrial survey. Whitman and Schmidt explain:

> GF's public relations program throughout the move was based on the following:
>
> 1. Full and early disclosure of all management decisions to employees and the public in that order
> 2. Involvement of top management through personal contacts with leaders in both the old and new plant communities

3. Continuing communication through bulletins from top management to the affected employees as well as continuing communication at the plant to assist each employee in deciding what was in his or her own best interest

4. Concern for the welfare of the affected communities and earnest attempts to ease the blow

5. Extensive efforts to establish sound relations with new employees and the new community[4]

(The two largest plants being closed, Hoboken and Dorchester, were unionized. The company consented to a National Labor Relations Board supervised election at the earliest possible date at the new plant, which the union won by a substantial majority.)

Once the Dover, Delaware, location was selected, General Foods began an active public relations program to prepare the community for the arrival of its people. At the same time, employees at the plants slated for closure were kept informed of the step-by-step progress, and as the time approached the company reiterated its pledge of a job for every employee who wanted to transfer—and for whom there was a job available—with expense-paid trips to Dover for employees and their families to look over the new area and locate a place to live. For those who did not want to move, termination allowances and assistance in finding employment were provided; these employees also received bonuses if they remained until the actual date of closing.

Of course, there was an engineering phase, too. General Foods used critical path models to plot plant and equipment layout decisions. The consolidation forced the company to ask such questions as: Should there be space for new products, and if so, how much? What technical improvements could be incorporated into the new plant? And from the financial side, comparisons had to be made between existing costs and costs at the new facilities, including profit and loss projections. The authors point out:

> Early studies can benefit from the use of top talent throughout the entire corporation, at least on a consulting basis. On the other hand, the more people who know of possible plant shutdowns, the greater the chance for news leaks and rumors and possible serious effects on employee morale at the old plants . . . the "need to know" criteria should be applied in deciding who should be told of the studies underway.
>
> Even though the early studies may indicate the desirability of building a new plant, there will naturally be some opposition to the closing of old plants. Such opposition may be based on sentiment rather than fact or upon the often present tendency to resist change. On the other hand, there are those who want to jump on the bandwagon in favor of the move on the theory that the new is always better than the old. Neither sentiment should be allowed to affect a logical examination of the facts and figures on which the decision must be based.[5]

A HEADQUARTERS RELOCATION

Faced with overcrowding in its general headquarters space in New York City and frustrated by the difficulty of communication between its senior executives, Johns-Manville Corporation decided to pack its bags and move the world headquarters to a cattle ranch outside Denver, Colorado. It was a major undertaking that ultimately involved the relocation of some 1150 employees and their families from the New York area.

As soon as the decision was made, it was announced.

Shortly thereafter, meetings of employees and their spouses were held in Manhattan and in Manville, New Jersey, where audio-visual presentations were made on Denver as a place to live. At the meetings were representatives of the Denver Chamber of Commerce, the Denver Board of Realtors (who discussed the resale housing market), the Home Builders Association (who discussed new housing construction costs and time frames), and the Board of Education (who talked about the various school districts and answered questions about special needs).

Next step was to schedule a trip to Denver for every employee asked to relocate. With all expenses paid, groups of ten employees were flown to Denver where they were housed at a first-class motel for a full week and provided a rental car. At the motel was a reception center with literature and a representative of the Home Builders and Realtors to answer questions and make appointments. Each evening, Johns-Manville sponsored an informal reception for the employees so that they could swap experiences and tell each other what they had learned about the schools, churches, neighborhoods, etc. The company arranged "bridge" financing on home purchases, furnished employment leads for the employee's spouse, and provided crash courses on everything from how long employees had to obtain automobile tags and the kind of test given for a driver's license to the tax liabilities they might incur.

When the time of the actual move came, Johns-Manville picked up virtually all moving costs, temporary living expenses, etc. Altogether the company spent about $23,000 per employee to move the employee and family plus transfer all the company files, records, furniture, data processing, etc. Total cost: $26 million.

When the relocation decision was made, Johns-Manville

decided that it would be best to get to Denver as soon as possible. As a result, the company located and rented interim space where some of the new concepts being considered—open space, interior landscaping design, bold use of color, secretarial pooling—could be tried without making a long-term commitment.

Another benefit that a significant relocation gives a company is the opportunity to improve its performance in perhaps the most difficult part of personnel management—getting rid of marginal employees. Not everyone has to be invited to move. These include those close to retirement age and those not contributing to the company's success or not important to future plans.

Johns-Manville found that the move West also heightened executive receptivity to new ideas and provided a great opportunity to reexamine every corporate action and every corporate policy.

NOTES

1. *Mini-Survey of New Hires and Group Moves*, Employee Relocation Council, August 1977.
2. William S. Gault, "Planning and Managing a Corporate Group Move," *The Personnel Administrator*, February 1978, pp. 31–41, 24.
3. James M. Keane, "Minimizing People Problems in a Group Move Situation," *The Personnel Administrator*, February 1978, pp. 42–44.
4. Edmund S. Whitman and W. James Schmidt, *Plant Relocation: A Case History of a Move*, American Management Associations, New York, 1966.
5. Ibid.

THIRTEEN

Special Problems of Foreign Firms

Prejudice still appears to be the number one concern of foreign nationals. "The Japanese and Germans are particularly sensitive," notes Richard S. Roberts, a senior international investment advisor in the Invest in the U.S.A. office of the U.S. Department of Commerce.

The Invest in the U.S.A. office is one of the first stops that a foreign investor should make when exploring the possibility of entering the United States market. Manned by Roberts, another advisor, and a secretary, this group seeks to attract foreign capital into the country.

Roberts lists five reasons why the Invest in the U.S.A. program is important to Americans: (1) it creates jobs; (2) it provides a transfer of foreign technology to our shores; (3) it acts to replace imports (made here, not there); (4) it makes for a broadening of the tax base at all levels (federal, state, and local); and (5) it helps to stabilize the United States dollar.

The Office of Foreign Investment, U.S. Department of Commerce, was set up in 1975 to keep track of what foreign companies are doing in the United States; thirty-five people collect and catalog the acquisitions, mergers, and equity activities of foreign investors. Milton A. Berger, director of that office, outlined the attraction of the United States to foreigners in a speech at the 1978 Spring meeting of the Society of Industrial Realtors:

The fact of the matter is that, however unfavorably foreigners view current U.S. approaches toward resolving its international payments and declining dollar problems, they recognize the inherent strength, stability and dynamism of the U.S. economy.

These are the fundamental reasons why foreigners are investing in the United States. We have been calling these "pull" factors—the vast expanding U.S. market, the free enterprise concept and the non-involvement of government, the availability of material and human resources, relative advantages in production costs, favorable investment policies at the federal and state levels, and relative labor and price stability. Abroad are the "push" factors—the desire to locate production in the United States in order to hold and expand positions in our market, uneasiness and political and economic stability in the home countries, growing governmental involvement in business activity, concern about labor participation in the management of business enterprises, fears over the possibility of U.S. restrictive import measures, interest in improving access to American technology, and the growing strength of foreign firms and confidence in their ability to operate on our terrain. And, of course, cost factors provide strong impetus to foreign investments at this time. Share prices are low, stimulating acquisition activity; and foreign investors contemplating new plant construction or expansion of existing facilities find their appreciated currencies will take them a long way at this time.

CHOOSING THE MARKET

"Almost all foreign firms are awed with the size of the market and have to be taught to break the U.S. up into regions and to think of the individual states as markets," notes Roberts. He encourages the foreign firm to select the market first and then think in more specific terms. "Concentrate on the marketing," he emphasizes, "if the product is fairly priced and a good product, it will sell."

A foreign investor deciding to establish or join an operating entity in the United States must weigh its own specific needs against the extraordinary size and diverse possibilities of the United States market, stresses the Bank of America in a brochure it distributes to the international investor. Entitled "Direct Investment in the United States from Abroad," the document provides an overview of the United States marketplace with estimates of growth rates of regional markets and of key industries:

> The United States offers an extraordinary number of combinations of markets (industrial, farm, extractive, consumer), products (machine tools, farm implements, mining machinery, textiles) and types of facilities (manufacturing, assembly, processing, warehousing, distribution/sales, service).
>
> Also, the country's vast physical size, its wide range of climatic and physical characteristics, the uneven geographic distribution of its population, and the diverse regional, ethnic, racial, and religious backgrounds represented among its people make it, for many purposes, a heterogeneous mar-

197

ket. . . . One highly significant consideration in the marketing area is whether the investor wishes to compete nationally or within one or more regional markets. Each regional market has its own characteristics of labor cost, population, income growth, and availability and cost of raw materials and power. And, as a general rule, companies confining investment activities to one or two regional markets can proceed with less capital than companies with national ambitions.[1]

From the foreign perspective, the quality of life does not vary a great deal from one part of the country to another, points out Roberts. Transportation and electrical supply are also generally good and usually not major considerations. The one relocation pitfall that manufacturers have to consider are environmental problems. Developers and environmentalists are at loggerheads, with the result that companies often have to opt for their second or third choice.

Labor concerns also rank high on the list of questions for which foreign companies need answers, continues Roberts. "We point out that while there currently exists a five to ten year labor cost advantage in the South that the wage differential is closing. Also, the labor unions in the South tend to extend a warmer welcome to new businesses. Generally speaking, in the North the labor unions are more intransigent. Roberts emphasizes:

> What we stress with the foreign firm is the security of the investment. Site selection, in our view, sits at the bottom of the inverted pyramid. When the company begins the search process, we try to encourage them to look at several locations, including some that many would not classify as the traditional place to invest. Spartanburg, South Carolina, for example, now has 30 foreign companies, mostly German,

and the town now has special festivals each year reflecting the heritage of its new inhabitants.

Sources of money are another concern of the foreign firm. The Invest in the U.S.A. office encourages a company to hire a private tax accountant and attorney because of the variation from state to state and the continuing evolution of the tax system.

REGULATORY CONSIDERATIONS

An aspect that seems difficult to grasp for foreigners looking at the United States market for the first time is that, in accordance with its free market system, the basic policy toward capital from abroad is to treat it on an equal basis with domestic capital. The intent of our laws, particularly anti-trust laws, is to foster open competition.

The foreign investor can own 100 percent of its United States affiliate, with no domestic company or governmental participation required as in many countries. In addition, the foreign investor does not have to register at the federal level, and there are no limitations or repatriations of capital or earnings. Of course, capital from countries such as North Vietnam and North Korea with whom our government does not have diplomatic relations cannot enter the United States freely.

Foreign investors also are excluded from or permitted only partial investment in: fresh water shipping; domestic radio, television, telephone and telegraph communications; domestic air transport; hydroelectric power; facilities for the utilization or production of atomic energy; and mining oper-

199

ations on lands owned by the federal government. Also, almost all states require foreign insurance companies to set up "trustee deposits" equal to the company's outstanding liabilities. And certain states deny aliens the right to engage in various aspects of the alcoholic beverage industry.

In general, a foreign company can organize a wholly owned subsidiary company under the various laws of a state. It can secure the benefits of limited liability through incorporation within a single state and then may do business in other states subject to each state's individual requirements. Some states do require that a specified number or percentage of incorporators or directors must be United States citizens.

Since the United States does not have any exchange control regulations, there are no restrictions on the flow of funds between the foreign parent and the United States subsidiary. Foreign firms wishing to offer securities must comply with the laws of the Securities and Exchange Commission that regulate any such public offering. The purpose of these laws is to ensure a full and fair disclosure of the nature of a security and to prevent fraud. Most states have securities laws as well.

Between January 1 and June 30, 1978, the U.S. Office of Foreign Investment identified 301 cases of foreign direct investment activity. Of these, 107 were in the form of completed or pending acquisitions or mergers. Investors from West Germany have been the most active, with 60 transactions, followed closely by those from the United Kingdom, with 56. The totals for the first six months of 1978 were up substantially from those of 1977, as can be seen in Table 26. The 66 percent of cases for which the value of the transaction was known for these first six months of 1977 accounted

TABLE 26   Foreign Direct Investment Activity in the United States

Country of Investor	January–June 1978 No. of completed/ pending cases	January–June 1977 No. of completed/ pending cases	No. cases value known	Value ($ million)
Belgium	4	10	3	24.5
Canada	43	22	14	711.0
France	14	12	7	283.9
Germany, F.R.	60	19	17	486.3
Italy	9	1	1	20.0
Japan	29	19	10	154.9
Netherlands	12	9	4	129.4
Switzerland	14	3	2	53.4
United Kingdom	56	22	17	342.9
Other	60	14	11	270.4
Total	301	131	86	2,476.7

SOURCE: Investment Analysis Division, Office of Foreign Investment in the United States, U.S. Department of Commerce.

for about $2.5 billion, which entered the United States as direct investment.

Generally speaking, says Commerce director Berger, manufacturing accounts for about two-fifths of all foreign investment, with another fifth in petroleum and another in trade. The remaining portion of foreign investment is in real estate, which in 1978 was valued at a little over $800 million but relates only to the real estate industry and does not include industrial land or plants owned by foreign-owned companies.

But foreign investors eying United States real estate need to be cautious. "It seems like there are 80 million American brokers offering their packages of property all over the world," says Jack Shaffer, senior vice president of the Sonnenblick-Goldman Corporation, a New York real estate company. "They fill up hotel lobbies wherever you go. Some of these guys are real estate people who would scare you and me and they've all got 'deals.'" Shaffer says he knew of two transactions involving shopping centers in ghetto areas—one near Atlanta, one in Los Angeles—that American investors would not touch at almost any price.

A CASE HISTORY

As with United States companies, once a foreign firm has made a decision to expand, the pressure intensifies to find a place and to get on with the move. Such was the case for Niro Atomizer, an international manufacturer of drying equipment with headquarters in Copenhagen, Denmark. The choice was made in two months after the search began. According to Niro Atomizer's President, Ole Andersen, five key items dictated the choice of location: (1) customer location; (2) availability of industrial bond financing; (3) adequate, easy-to-finance housing for employees; (4) availability of qualified professional and technical personnel; and (5) access to airports.

Since the chemical industry is a very important customer, says Anderson, that meant a location on the East Coast. After discussions with the Commerce departments of several states, the choice was narrowed to three cities: Danbury, Connecticut; Camden, New Jersey; and Columbia, Maryland. The choice of Columbia was actually made by the eleven European employees involved in the move after visiting the three sites. "The concept of Columbia had a definite impact on our final decision," adds Andersen. (The Scandinavian countries have built several "new towns" similar to Columbia, mostly on the outskirts of major cities.)

Niro Atomizer started construction in 1975 and moved in in April of 1976. Current professional employment numbers around 150, out of which 100 to 110 are chemical or mechanical engineers, and land has been bought for additional expansion. The Columbia site serves as the center for design and engineering, with some pilot plant work. Actual construction of the equipment takes place under a number of subcontracts; several of the subcontractors are located in the Baltimore area.

COMMON GOALS

Apart from the special problem of finding a place where foreign nationals will feel comfortable, the needs of the foreign company and the domestic company seeking a site have more similarities in common than differences.

Manufacturing companies have to consider the availability of raw materials, the nearness to markets and key customers, and the composition of the area's labor force. Distribution companies want to maximize the customer base and minimize transportation costs. And regional offices, R&D facilities, and headquarters offices have as their top priorities the availability of executive professional talent and the ease of moving people to troubleshoot for, or communicate with, other parts of the company and customers.

Once several locations have been selected which meet the basic criteria established before the search began, then secondary factors come into play—the ease of obtaining financing, the level of local and state taxes, the cost of utilities, and other items that lend themselves to numerical comparisons.

Unfortunately, many locations decision makers stop their analysis at this point. They virtually ignore the people side of the equation. By so doing, they can create a situation where the educational, social, and cultural environment as well as housing, recreation, and other quality-of-life factors may be such that the facility never achieves the targeted product output and quality, marketing goals, or creativity needs.

Both domestic and foreign companies should use logic and business facts to narrow the list of location possibilities. But in the end, it's the people who live and work at the new location who will determine in large measure the "success" of the site.

What we have been stressing throughout this book is the fact that companies can make a serious mistake when only the head is involved in the selection process and the heart is left out. Niro Atomizer let its key employees who would be making the move select from three alternatives. Domestic companies can learn from their example. Only when *both* objective and subjective factors receive proper weighting, we believe, will the site achieve and surpass management's expectations.

NOTES

1. *Direct Investment in the United States from Abroad: A Bank of America Survey for the International Investor*, World Banking Division, Bank of America NT&SA, New York, 1978. All rights reserved. Reprinted by permission.

2. Michael Goodwin, "Everybody's Getting In on Foreign Investor Action," *The New York Times*, section 8, July 2, 1978, pp. 1, 4.

FOURTEEN

Pitfalls
and Pointers

The decision maker often looks only at differences in the price of land, the cost and availability of labor, the cost of utilities, tax considerations, and other easily compared numbers. As a result, it's tempting for the searcher to rely just on these and to ignore analysis of the subjective characteristics of a site. Yet it is the quality-of-life factors that not only determine the happiness (and often productivity) of key employees but also provide some measure of the business environment which the company will probably be a part of for at least twenty years.

Many companies take the position that they need not be concerned about the amenities a community offers since they will hire the bulk of the work force locally. Nonetheless, a cadre of management people is likely to be transferred to the new location, and others may need to be recruited from outside the community. The ability to attract and keep the best people will depend largely on whether the money offered and/or the opportunity for advancement can offset the location's daily unpleasantries, possible disadvantages in education for the children, and other shortcomings.

Another factor of critical importance in optimizing success at a site is the community's attitude. Companies often assume that they and their people will be welcomed simply because they will bring new jobs to the community. While that conclusion would have been generally true just a few years ago, it no longer holds true in many communities. In fact, the more desirable the community, the more likely that the community's leaders (and its residents) will believe that they can pick and choose among *all* of the companies that are expanding or relocating. Even where public officials welcome a new company, the company may find that others in the community are not so overjoyed. Frequently the reason is selfish—the existing businesses don't want employees lured away by higher wages or better working conditions. The likely opponents in a community should be uncovered before the company fully commits itself to a site.

An unfortunate fact of life is that communities still exist which practice a very real form of discrimination against various religious and ethnic groups. Even some very large communities may be closed (with respect to luncheon clubs or country clubs) to graduates of certain colleges or universities or to those whose ancestral roots are planted elsewhere.

Geographical discrimination can also exist. For no rational reason, some Southerners do not like "Yankees," New Englanders may not care for Midwesterners, and those living on the West Coast may resent the invasion of Easterners who will "despoil their paradise."

It is unlikely that the persons making a site search will encounter these attitudes when talking with the official representative of a community or a local developer. That's why it's important that the person in charge of the site selection conduct an incognito, independent examination of the real attitudes prevalent in a community.

The political climate of a community should also be investigated. Which political party has control is unimportant; what is important can be an erratic political history and particularly one where the politicians use business as the whipping boy. Back issues of the local newspaper can provide insights into local issues, such as "no growth" movements and how they were handled.

Affirmative Action and other Equal Employment Opportunity (EEO) programs should be examined when considering a relocation or expansion. Recently, some companies planning a move from a major city to its suburbs have found themselves the target of litigation. The purpose of the legal action has been to prevent corporations from moving their business to "lily-white" areas difficult for minorities to reach. If the motive of the move is to escape from an integrated community, perhaps the company should go back to the drawing board on both moral and business grounds. Thomas Johnson, vice president-administration of Concordia Publishing House in St. Louis, points out that it is essential for a corporation to locate in an area where either the population is currently integrated or where there is sufficient access to transportation for workers at the lower end of the economic scale.[1]

H. McKinley Conway, Jr., president of Conway Research, points out that a particular state's "good package of incentive programs" can be nullified by "overzealous administration of environmental regulations and other controls."[2] He observes that industrial real estate decisions should be made at the lowest level of government possible and that the way to avoid costly and time-consuming duplication is to consolidate project approvals.

The Dow Chemical Company's abandonment of efforts to obtain environmental clearances for construction of a $500 million petrochemical complex in California has several lessons for the location decision maker. The site Dow chose was a remote 2800-acre section of Solano County with a record of poor farming productivity—only $60/acre income annually. Dow bought the land after it obtained an approved state-level Environmental Impact Report (EIR) in early 1976. After two years of effort at a cost of $4 million plus $6 million for the land, the California state agencies decided to rewrite the EIR, which meant starting the clearance process all over again. As a result, Dow decided to withdraw its plan for construction.

> What did Dow learn? Raymond I. Brubaker, Jr., general manager of the Western division of Dow Chemical U.S.A., suggests two lessons:
> (1) For projects of this magnitude, there is a very high degree of uncertainty as to how the regulations will be administered by governmental administrators;
> (2) There was and is a substantial amount of uncertainty with respect to public policy regarding industrial growth, especially in California. . . . . We were naive to assume that because we had gotten across the first hurdle of the EIR we were safe. We bought the land too quickly. An option would have been wiser.[3]

A recent research report by the Industrial Development Research Council supports the necessity of caution when dealing in environmental matters. Entitled "A Composite Case History of New Facility Location," the report is based on recent experiences in locating seventy-seven manufacturing, warehouse, and office projects for some of the nation's leading industrial firms. Two of the findings seem particularly appropriate: In the area of environmental regulation, water and air quality control were the source of most of the delays and expenses for manufacturers, while land use issues were the biggest environmental factors for warehouses and offices. Further, less than half of the seventy-seven participants in the study reported a need for backup systems or an alternate energy plan. Only two companies investigated independent energy sources and none indicated an interest in the "energy park" concept. (In an energy park, several companies cooperate to build an energy center for their mutual needs.) Suggests *Industrial Development* magazine:

> There are probably several reasons for the apparent lack of concern about energy alternatives. First, there may be a time lag between identification of a "crisis" issue and the response to that "crisis" in facility planning. Second, it is possible that some companies don't believe there is an energy crisis, or perhaps they feel that energy is not a critical component of the total facility. It is also possible that it may not be economically feasible to develop energy alternatives, particularly for the small to medium-sized plants which comprise the majority of the case histories in the study. A more likely answer, however, is that industry's principal response to the energy shortage is to locate facilities in an area where there is a secure supply of energy and thus obviate the need for alternatives.[4]

If you are planning a sizable plant with considerable amounts of traffic moving into and out of the plant, it would be smart to go to the county planning engineer's office and look over the plans for circumferential highways, arterial highways, bypass highways, and so forth. A plant should be located to take advantage of both the existing and planned transportation network.

Another point in the transportation area that could prove important for many companies is the intermodal shipping capabilities. The trend is toward containers that can be moved by air, ship, rail, and truck. Have you, or should you, restructure your shipping to take advantage of intermodal transfer? And what about the nearness to an air transportation operation—not a receiver but an actual shipper? Finally, if you ship a number of small packages, have you located the nearest bulk shipping terminal of the Post Office Department? Locating outside the area of such a shipping terminal could prove a foolish and costly decision for those who rely on the postal service to deliver their products to the customer.

There is an additional check that you should make before finalizing the selection. Take a walk around the community. See what condition the streets and sidewalks are in. Look at the houses and churches—are they painted and well-kept? Do the schools and other public buildings look run down? Keep remembering that most of the workers will come from the community, and if the community has no pride in its appearance, then the workers may have little pride in their work, and productivity at your facility will reflect that.

Finally, ask yourself these questions. If the company transferred me to this location, would I want to move my family here? Where would we live, shop, go to church? What would we do for recreation, entertainment? If *you* would think twice before taking the transfer, maybe you should think twice before recommending the site.

THE ACTUAL MOVE

As the day approaches for the physical transfer of files and other office equipment from the old to the new location, several details remain for the executive overseeing the move. Apart from making sure that new employees have been properly screened and trained, be certain that contractors have been hired (or employees trained) to provide the services you will need—heating and electricity, landscaping, janitorial functions, security, fire protection, and medical help. And don't forget to lay in a sufficient inventory of needed supplies or materials to hold you through the break-in period.

One more administrative detail remains before you put your people and equipment into the new facility. Make sure that the necessary insurance has been secured. This includes policies for fire, fidelity bonds, workmen's compensation, liability, and theft.

Now it's moving time. If there are less than 500 people involved, an experienced moving company should be able to transfer the physical equipment over a weekend. And if you have properly marked all the equipment for the new location and have given specific directions to each employee as to where he or she will be located, then come Monday it should be business as usual. But if you don't want to start off with broken equipment and a few other unpleasantries, just take one last check (Figure 19).

FIG. 19 Moving your office, right and wrong: Suggestions. from a moving company to facilitate the move. (SOURCE: Kenneth H. Ripnen, *Office Space Administration*, McGraw-Hill, New York, 1974, p. 143.)

It's WRONG to do the following:

- It's wrong to overload boxes to point of overflowing. Use extra box or container instead.

- It's wrong to forget to tag every item. If an item comes apart, tag each part or section separately with the same number.

- It's wrong to leave your personal belongings such as money, lighters, fountain pens, snap shots etc. in your desk. Take them with you to your new location.

- It's wrong to place boxes or containers on the desks where they might scratch the surface. Leave them on the floor next to the desk where they can be conveniently moved by the mover.

It is imperative that movers have as much room to operate in as possible and it is our suggestion that only absolutely necessary personnel remain on the premises during the moving operation. Your moving cost can be materially reduced by efficient, split second timing and intelligent cooperation from each and every person. Moving day can be like any other business day, if you merely observe the following recommendations:

RIGHT

Desks. Wherever possible desks will be moved with contents. Loose papers should be banded or placed in large clasp type envelopes. When moving, desks are turned on end to be taken out of rooms.

Desk Accessories. Desk lights, inter office communication systems or any other electrical equipment not requiring the services of an electrician should merely be disconnected from the electric socket and properly

---

tagged using the number provided in the floor plan. Telephones attached to desks should be disconnected in advance.

Liquids. Inks, mucilage, rubber cement and any other liquids should be removed from desks, cabinets and files. Be certain all tops, corks and stoppers are tight. Place in waste baskets or box.

Files. Contents of file should remain intact with file guards drawn as tight as possible. Lock file if possible. Files will be moved upright whenever possible. Files fastened together will be separated by movers and replaced in new location according to plan.

Cardex files. Rods and guards must be tightened as much as possible to hold contents securely. If there are loose cards, they should be banded together in packs of about 200.

Typewriters. Typewriters should be removed from desks and left on tops of desks. Tag typewriter with same number as desk. Typewriter will be placed in special typewriter box by the mover. Carriages should be securely tied.

Stationery Cabinets and Steel Shelving. Contents should be packed in boxes provided. Tag boxes with same number as stationery cabinet or steel shelving unit.

Glass Tops. Leave glass top on desk but tag with same number as desk. Remove paper or loose felt from under glass and place in desk drawer.

Pictures—Maps. Large pictures and maps should be tagged with new location numbers as indicated on floor plan and left on walls: small pictures should be removed from walls and placed in boxes marked with room numbers. All flat glass objects should be placed in boxes on end and not laid flat.

Loose Casters. If there are desks or chairs with loose casters, please remove same and place in desk drawer.

NOTES

1. "City or Suburb—Which Is Best for an Office Site?" *Administrative Management*, Octorber 1977, pp. 28–32.

2. "Rating the States on Cooperativeness," *Industry Week*, June 23, 1975, pp. 21–22.

3. Raymond I. Brubaker, Jr., "A Rocky Road Awaits Industry on Its Way Through the Environmental Obstacle Course," *Industrial Development* March/April 1978, pp. 2–5. (Quoted by permission of Conway Publications, Inc., Atlanta, Georgia.)

4. "New IDRC Research Report Probes Facility Planning Factors," reproduced from *Industrial Development*, May/June 1978, pp. 32–33, by permission of Conway Publications, Inc., Atlanta, Georgia. No further reproduction is permitted.

APPENDIX

Recommended Reading List for the CID Examination *

1. *The Practice of Industrial Development,* Howard D Bessire. Published by the Hill Printing Company, P.O. Box 515, El Paso, Texas 79942. 915/542-1611. Also available from the AIDC Educational Foundation, P.O. Box 474, South Hamilton, Massachusetts 01982.

2. *The Developers' Dictionary and Handbook,* Koder M. Collison. Published by Lexington Books, 125 Spring Street, Lexington, Massachusetts 02173.

3. *Bringing in the Sheaves,* John R. Fernstrom. Available from the Extension Business Office, Extension Hall, Oregon State University, Corvallis, Oregon 97331.

4. *Industrial Development: Concepts and Principles,* Henry L. Hunker. Published by Lexington Books, 125 Spring Street, Lexington, Massachusetts 02173. Also available from the AIDC Educational Foundation, P.O. Box 474, South Hamilton, Massachusetts 01982.

5. *Industrial Development Handbook.* Sponsored by the Executive Group of the Industrial Council of ULI— the Urban Land Institute. Available from the Urban

*Candidates for the Certified Industrial Developer examination must be graduates of the Industrial Development Institute at the University of Oklahoma.

Land Institute, 1200 18th Street, N.W., Washington, D.C. 20036.

6. *Industrial Real Estate* (2d ed.), William N. Kinnard, Jr., and Stephen D. Messner, Society of Industrial Realtors®, 1300 Connecticut Avenue, N.W., Washington, D.C. 20036.

7. *Industrial Facilities Planning.* Published by Conway Publications, Inc., 1954 Airport Road, Atlanta, Georgia 30341.

8. *Bibliography of State-Directed Research for Economic Development, 1970–1976,* Available from the United States Department of Commerce, Economic Development Administration, Office of Economic Research, Washington, D.C. 20230. Also available from the National Technological Information Service, 5285 Port Royal Road, Springfield, Virginia 22161,—special ordering instructions—request PB 267771, cost $9.00 (payment must be sent with order).

9. *Principles of Industrial Development,* Richard Preston (ed.). Available from the AIDC Educational Foundation, Post Office Box 474, South Hamilton, Massachusetts 01982.

10. *The Universe of Industrial Development and North American Concepts and Practice* (revised). Published by the American Industrial Development Council, Inc., 215 West Pershing Road, Suite 707, Kansas City, Missouri 64108.

11. *AIDC Annotated Bibliography.* Published by the American Industrial Development Council, Inc., 215 West Pershing Road, Suite 707, Kansas City, Missouri 64108.

Index

Access, 149
Adam, Everett E., Jr., 13
Addresses:
  Census Bureau, U.S., 151
  for consultants, 21
Administrative costs at present
  and proposed site, 51
Affirmative action, 207
Agglomeration factors in location
  theory, 54
Air transportation:
  available, 18
  checklist on questions of, 28
"All American City" (designation),
  96
American City Corporation, 50
American City and County, The
  (publication), 37
Andersen, Ole, 202

Baltimore Gas & Electric Company
  (BG&E), 73, 76, 77
Bank of America, 197–198
Banks, financing assistance from,
  141
Berger, Milton A., 196, 201
Big cities (*see* Cities)
Blacks:
  and companies in the Sunbelt,
    96–97
  migration of, 93, 94
Bonded indebtedness, 17
Breckenfeld, Gurney, 96–97, 101,
  103–104
Brubaker, Raymond I., Jr., 208
Bureau of Economic Analysis (U.S.
  Department of Commerce), 35
Bureau of International Com-
  merce (U.S. Department of
  Commerce), 65
Bureau of Labor Statistics (U.S.
  Department of Labor), 69

Business climate factors in site
  selection, 46, 108
Business and Industrial Develop-
  ment, Division of (Department
  of Economic and Community
  Development, Maryland),
  39–40
Business loan programs, state (*see*
  States, business loan pro-
  grams of)
"Business Loves the Sunbelt (and
  Vice Versa)" (Breckenfeld), 90
Business Week (magazine), 34, 35

Carroll, Thomas M., 152
Carter, Jimmy, 37
Census Bureau, U.S., 151
Certified Industrial Developers
  (CID), 20–21
Certified Industrial Developers
  Examination, 215–216
Chase, Marilyn, 96
Cities:
  big, as potential sites, 89–97
  energy cost in major, 73–75
    table, 74–75
  growth and tax rates of, 155
  and new towns, 101–105
  population of, 89, 93
    tables, 90, 94
  (*See also* Population)
  relocation and decline of, 10
  revitalization of, 95–97
  size of, as determinant of prefer-
    red location, 115–116
  small, as potential sites, 99–100
  theories on structure of, 88–89
  transportation and communica-
    tion facilities undermining,
    as sites, 10–11
  varying home values in, as de-
    terrent to relocation, 121

217